CONFRONTING
RACIAL INJUSTICE

CONFRONTING RACIAL INJUSTICE

THEORY *and* PRAXIS
for the CHURCH

GERALD HIESTAND *and*
JOEL LAWRENCE, *editors*

 CASCADE *Books* • Eugene, Oregon

CONFRONTING RACIAL INJUSTICE
Theory and Praxis for the Church

The Center for Pastor Theologians Series

Cascade Books
An Imprint of Wipf and Stock Publishers
199 W. 8th Ave., Suite 3
Eugene, OR 97401

www.wipfandstock.com

PAPERBACK ISBN: 978-1-6667-3734-9
HARDCOVER ISBN: 978-1-6667-9666-7
EBOOK ISBN: 978-1-6667-9667-4

Cataloguing-in-Publication data:

Names: Hiestand, Gerald, 1974–, editor. | Lawrence, Joel, editor.

Title: Confronting racial injustice: theory and praxis for the church / edited by Gerald Hiestand and Joel Lawrence.

Description: Eugene, OR : Cascade Books, 2022 | Series: The Center for Pastor Theologians Series | Includes bibliographical references and index.

Identifiers: ISBN 978-1-6667-3734-9 (paperback) | ISBN 978-1-6667-9666-7 (hardcover) | ISBN 978-1-6667-9667-4 (ebook)

Subjects: LCSH: Race relations—Religious aspects—Christianity. | Ethnic relations—Religious aspects—Christianity. | Reconciliation—Religious aspects—Christianity. | United States—Race relations.

Classification: E184.A1 C653 2022 (paperback) | E184.A1 C653 (ebook)

VERSION NUMBER 110122

To the scholars and thought leaders of color who made possible the conference that inspired this volume:

Vincent Bacote

Raymond Chang

Charlie Dates

Ernest Gray

Kiem Le

Esau McCaulley

Winfred Omar Neely

Neal D. Presa

Eric C. Redmond

Michelle Ami Reyes

Paul Sanchez

Love Lazarus Sechrest

Contents

Part One: Exegetical Theology

Part Two: Ecclesial Theology

Part Three: Contextual Theology

Acknowledgments

As in the past, we owe a debt of gratitude to the contributors of this volume. The subject of racial injustice—and the church's engagement (and complicity) with it—is a matter of pressing kingdom concern. We are grateful for the many able women and men who have thought, and continue to think, deeply on this important issue.

Likewise, we are grateful to the Center for Pastor Theologians (CPT), the organizer of the conference from which the papers of this book are drawn. The center has served as a catalyst for our work and has been a repository of wisdom and counsel on all things pastoral and theological. The staff of the center—Todd Wilson (president), Joel Lawrence (executive director), Rae Paul (managing director), and Zach Wagner (editorial director) did a tremendous job organizing the 2021 conference, and we deeply value their ongoing work on behalf of the mission and vision of the CPT.

In the same spirit, we are deeply grateful for the partnership of the CPT's five senior theological mentors: Scott Hafemann, Doug Sweeney, Peter Leithart, Kevin Vanhoozer, and Timothy George. Their commitment to the CPT's mission, their contribution to the fellowships, and their friendship and encouragement to the two of us have been important catalysts for the CPT project and its associated publications.

Likewise, we continue to be profoundly grateful for Calvary Memorial Church in Oak Park, Illinois, the congregation where CPT cofounders Todd Wilson and Gerald Hiestand have been privileged to serve as pastors. Calvary has graciously served as the host home for the CPT for more than a decade, and it is not an overstatement to say that the CPT would not be what it is without Calvary's partnership and support. The use of Calvary's building, the help from Calvary's staff, and the support of Calvary's elder council have been tremendous resources for the CPT.

And finally, we owe Myndi Lawrence a special debt of gratitude for her labors as our chief copy and production editor for this volume. Myndi did a tremendous job in organizing, copyediting, chasing down missing citations, and indexing, in order to produce a completed manuscript ready for submission.

Abbreviations

CM   Colonial mentality

CPT   Center for Pastor Theologians

CRT   Critical race theory

ICC   International Critical Commentary

JBL   *Journal of Biblical Literature*

JSPL   *Journal for the Study of Paul and His Letters*

LNTS   The Library of New Testament Studies

NCBC   New Cambridge Bible Commentary

NICNT   New International Commentary on the New Testament

NICOT   New International Commentary on the Old Testament

NovT   *Novum Testamentum*

NovTSup   Supplements to Novum Testamentum

NPNF1   Augustine. *Anti-Pelagian Writings*. Edited by Philip Schaff. Nicene and Post-Nicene Fathers, ser. 1, 5. Edinburgh: T. & T. Clark, 1997.

NPNF2   Athanasius. *Select Works and Letters*. Edited by Philip Schaff and Henry Wace. Nicene and Post-Nicene Fathers, ser. 2, 4. Peabody, MA: Hendrickson, 2004.

SNTSMS   Society for New Testament Studies Monograph Series

TNTC   Tyndale New Testament Commentaries

TOTC   Tyndale Old Testament Commentaries

Introduction

The Church's Crisis of Racial Injustice

GERALD HIESTAND *and* JOEL LAWRENCE, *editors*

FOR NEARLY A DECADE, the Center for Pastor Theologians (CPT) has gathered our network of pastors, friends in the academy, and lay church leaders for a three-day theology conference in Oak Park, Illinois. This gathering is unique in that it is neither an academic or denominational conference, nor is it focused on the pragmatics of church leadership. Rather, it is a theology conference for pastors and ministry leaders; a gathering focused on equipping pastors to be theologians for today's complex world. The conference flows from the CPT's mission to recenter theology in the church and to encourage pastors in their vocation as the primary theologians of the church.

Gathering in October 2021, the sixth CPT Conference came at a time of crisis for American Evangelicalism. The events of 2020 seemed almost intentionally designed to lay bare the church's idols and exploit the weaknesses inherent in evangelical culture. These fissures are now plain for all to see and demand the sustained theological work of the church's pastors in order to bring the body of Christ to a place of repentance and healing.

One of the greatest crises facing the church is the crisis of racial injustice that has so long marred the body of Christ in America. Evangelicals have traditionally had a set of biblical, theological, and cultural tools we have used for dealing with questions about race: the necessity of personal responsibility, the possibility of heart renewal through faith in Jesus, the transformative impact of interpersonal relationships, and the bedrock conviction that every human being is made in the image of God (*imago Dei*) and is thus of equal worth and dignity. But in the world after 2020, the evangelical church must now recognize that our theological playbook has been ineffective in rooting out racism from the church; what's more, it has been ineffective in confronting our own complicity with racial injustice. We must now ask: What other theological convictions are required of us as we consider the image-bearing humanity of George Floyd, Breonna Taylor, and Ahmaud Arbery, among many others?

American Evangelicals, regrettably, are not known for offering penetrating analyses of difficult subjects. When it comes to racial injustice, this tendency has not served us well. At the 2021 conference, we attempted to engage these issues differently. We were not on the hunt for easy answers or quick solutions. What easy answers could there be to questions about critical race theory or the political, sociological, and theological implications of the phrase "Black Lives Matter?" Instead, we wanted to delve into the challenges of how the evangelical church can prophetically and charitably engage in conversations about reparations, mass incarceration, historic patterns of racism, and white privilege. For the church to reclaim our witness to God's justice and righteousness, for the church to witness to Christ's unifying work across the tribal lines of worldly categorization, for the church to be an expression of the unity and diversity of our triune God, we must be prepared for the deep theological work that real progress necessarily entails. We must do this, because what is required is a humble, sober-minded, serious, and sacrificial reflection on the issue of race and the challenges (and opportunities) it presents. We must also be ready to trace the deep implications of these insights into our own lives, congregations, and communities—all for the glory of Jesus Christ.

The essays contained in this volume are written by people who have a shared love of Jesus Christ and a shared commitment to see his church be a faithful witness to the gospel. Our union in Christ is what binds us to one another. At the same time, these essays are written by people from a variety of racial, ethnic, and socioeconomic backgrounds whose perspectives are shaped by those experiences. In this, there is difference, disagreement, challenge, and confrontation, all of which necessitates a humble engagement with the work of the Spirit in our lives. As we prepared for the conference in a time in which it is so difficult to have healthy, mature, and productive conversations, our prayer was that it would be a gathering where God's people could truly listen, learn, and be challenged, and do so in an atmosphere shaped by the unity of the Spirit and the bond of peace.

It was also our prayer that white evangelical Christians, like ourselves, would humbly sit at the feet of our brothers and sisters of color, hearing their stories, seeing Christ, the church, and our world from their perspective. If the evangelical church is going to be healed of our racism, then white pastors will need to learn to follow, to humble themselves in the sight of the Lord and in the presence of our brothers and sisters of color who can be God's instrument of our own healing and of the healing of the body of Christ.

As you read these essays, we pray that you are moved by the Holy Spirit to compassion, repentance, humility, and the hard work of racial reconciliation. May God in his grace renew his church through the confession of sin and the ministry of his people, that we might be the answer to Jesus's prayer that we would be one, even as he and his Father are one.

Contributors

Vincent Bacote (PhD, Drew University) is professor of theology and director of the Center for Applied Christian Ethics at Wheaton College in Wheaton, Illinois. Publications include the books *Reckoning with Race and Performing the Good News: In Search of a Better Evangelical Theology* and *The Political Disciple: A Theology of Public Life*. He has also contributed to books such as *Cultural Engagement: A Crash Course in Contemporary Issues*.

Raymond Chang (MDiv, Trinity Evangelical Divinity School) is president of the Asian American Christian Collaborative, a pastor, and a writer. He regularly preaches God's word and speaks throughout the country on issues pertaining to Christianity and culture, race and faith, while serving as a campus minister at Wheaton College. He is currently pursuing his PhD.

Gerald Hiestand (PhD, University of Reading) is senior pastor at Calvary Memorial Church in Oak Park, Illinois, and the cofounder and board chair of the Center for Pastor Theologians. He is the coauthor of *The Pastor Theologian: Resurrecting an Ancient Vision* and coeditor of *Becoming a Pastor Theologian: New Possibilities for Church Leadership*.

Winfred Omar Neely (PhD, University of Aberdeen) is vice president and dean of Moody Theological Seminary and Graduate School. Formerly a missionary to Senegal, West Africa, he teaches in the department of Applied Theology and Church Ministries. In addition to contributing to the *Moody Handbook of Preaching*, he is the author of *How to Overcome Worry: Experiencing the Peace of God in Every Situation*.

Amy Peeler (PhD, Princeton Theological Seminary) is associate professor of New Testament at Wheaton College, Illinois, and associate rector at St. Mark's

Episcopal Church in Geneva, Illinois. Author of *"You Are My Son": The Family of God in the Epistle to the Hebrews*, she will release *Women and the Gender of God* in 2022.

Madison N. Pierce (PhD, Durham University) is assistant professor of New Testament at Trinity Evangelical Divinity School and an active member in the Anglican Church in North America. Her most recent publications are a book on the characterization of God through quotations in Hebrews, *Divine Discourse in the Epistle to the Hebrews*, and an edited collection on gospel origins and reception, *Gospel Reading and Reception in Early Christian Literature*.

Neal D. Presa (PhD, Drew University) is associate director of doctoral studies and visiting associate professor of preaching at New Brunswick Theological Seminary. Additionally, he is senior visiting professor of Union Theological Seminary (Philippines), adjunct professor of practical theology at International Theological Seminary (West Covina, California), research fellow of practical and missional theology of the University of the Free State (Bloemfontein, South Africa), and a CPT fellow. His seventh book is *Worship, Justice, and Joy: A Liturgical Pilgrimage* (forthcoming).

Eric C. Redmond (PhD, Capital Seminary and Graduate School) is professor of Bible at Moody Bible Institute, Chicago, and associate pastor of preaching, teaching, and care at Calvary Memorial Church, Oak Park, Illinois. His most recent publications include a chapter on hermeneutics in *One Volume Seminary* and the introduction to Ephesians in the *Tyndale House Greek New Testament, Guided, Annotated Reader's Edition* (forthcoming).

Michelle Ami Reyes (PhD, University of Illinois Chicago) is vice president of the Asian American Christian Collaborative and scholar-in-residence at Hope Community Church, Austin, Texas. She is the author of *Becoming All Things: How Small Changes Lead to Lasting Connections across Cultures*, as well as a co-author of the forthcoming book *The Race-Wise Family*.

Paul Sanchez (PhD, Southern Baptist Theological Seminary) is a Baptist pastor and has served churches in California and North Carolina. As a historian and theologian, his research has been focused on American religious history, with particular interest in Baptist history, theological liberalism, and Christian spirituality. He is a member of the St. John Fellowship at the Center for Pastor Theologians.

Love Lazarus Sechrest (PhD, Duke University) is associate provost and professor of theology at Mount St. Mary's University. Studying womanist and African American biblical interpretation and New Testament ethics, she is the author of *A Former Jew: Paul and the Dialectics of Race*; *Can "White" People be Saved? Triangulating Race, Theology, and Mission*; and *Race and Rhyme: Rereading the New Testament*.

Daniel (Danny) T. Slavich (PhD, Midwestern Seminary) is an ordained Southern Baptist pastor and church planter. He has been an adjunct professor at multiple institutions in South Florida in the area of theology and biblical studies. He has written in many places on the subjects of race, ethnicity, and multiethnic ecclesiology, including "In Church as It Is in Heaven" in the *Midwestern Journal of Theology*.

Gregory Thompson (PhD, University of Virginia) is a scholar, producer, writer, and cook who currently serves as the executive director of *Voices Underground*, an organization that pursues racial healing through collaborative storytelling. He co-authored the book *Reparations: A Christian Call for Repentance and Repair*.

Part One

EXEGETICAL THEOLOGY

1

The Perils of Passing

*Code-Switching and Intercultural Competency
in Acts*

Love Lazarus Sechrest

INTRODUCTION

DID YOU KNOW THAT "hair is political?" It is a truism among Black[1] women that hairstyles communicate politics, a powerful proverb linked to the fact that hair texture is one of the physical features that define blackness. Women especially end up making political choices about styling their hair: should they conform with the dictates of the hair's natural state, or should they appear in public in ways that conform to beauty standards keyed to White women? In 2010, Chastity Jones interviewed for a customer service representative job in Alabama, dressed in a business suit and pumps with her hair styled in natural locks, disparagingly known as "dreadlocks." Although she received an offer,

---

1. In this essay, I capitalize words that refer to subpopulations by race or ethnicity. This practice is ubiquitous in our society when referring to Asian-, Latinx-, Irish-, and Native Americans, etc., but contested when capitalizing White, when referring to that group of Americans. For more on this topic, see Nguyễn and Pendleton, "Recognizing Race in Language."

an HR manager nevertheless told her that she could not wear locks at work because they "tend to get messy." In other words, they violated the company's grooming policy. When Jones refused to cut her locks, the company withdrew the job offer.[2] According to some observers, something similar happened to Gabrielle Union in 2019 when she was allegedly asked to leave her job as a host on NBC's *America's Got Talent* because her hairstyles were "too Black."[3] In 2021, it was still legal in thirty-nine states for employers to fire workers for their hairstyles.

The news story about the Black male teen Andrew Johnson who was forced to cut his locks before a wrestling match was equally heartbreaking. He faced a political choice no teenager should have to make: fight to have his identity recognized or forfeit the match, losing up to six points for his team.[4] That child faced enormous public pressure from his coach and teammates to comply with rules that work in White culture but weren't created with someone like him in mind. Imagine how humiliating it was to have someone groom you in public for an alien set of cultural demands.

However, if these stories raise questions about *coercive* requests to assimilate to the dominant culture, the case of Rachel Dolezal represents a different kind of peril. Dolezal is a White woman in Spokane, Washington, who created a Black identity for herself.[5] She was a local BLM (Black Lives Matter) activist and taught Africana studies at Eastern Washington University, rising to become the president of the local chapter of the NAACP (National Association for the Advancement of Colored People). With a degree in art from the historically Black college Howard University, Dolezal insists that she is Black. She identifies with the Black experience in the US, despite having White parents and White features, notwithstanding the box braids or kinky blond wigs she often sported. Over the years, she carefully perpetuated her lie of Black identity through fraudulent documents and narratives until the day she was outed by a reporter. Afterward, she changed her name to a Nigerian name, Nkechi Amare Diallo, earning a living by braiding hair. Apparently, no one wants to hire a person to teach Black history who is neither credentialed in the subject nor acquainted with it as a matter of life experience. She sees herself as someone who successfully "passed" as Black and creates a hopeful space for other Whites to do the same, thus reducing White supremacy. In contrast, Black women see this as just another story

2. For more on civil rights, the politics of African American hair, and the case of Chastity Jones, see Griffin, "How Natural Black Hair"; A. Campbell, "Black Woman Lost."

3. Young, "Gabrielle Union."

4. Singer, "What Andrew Johnson Endured"; also see Andone, "Varsity Wrestler."

5. Oluo, "Heart of Whiteness"; St. Félix, "'Rachel Divide' Review."

of White entitlement gone awry. They ask, "Why not just be a great White ally?"

I suggest that all these cases involve emotionally charged decisions about identity and the loyalties that emerge from those identities. The women's situations involved stereotyped associations around a Black physical feature—hair socially constructed as messy, unkempt, unclean, and wild. The teenager's case tested his loyalties to two different "tribes" as he was asked to choose between his all-White wrestling team and his public appearance as an African American. The idea of sublimating one's ethnic identity to the dominant culture identity to avoid harm so that one "passes" for White is a profoundly painful topic in the African American community. Passing or otherwise aligning with outsider groups is a rejection of one's people and calls into question one's loyalty. On the other hand, the Rachel Dolezal case raises questions about agency and authenticity. Who gets to speak for a given people or tribe? Are Blacks unable to speak for themselves? Is Black identity a commodity that can be adopted at will?

I contend that intercultural competence can help us navigate this terrain. This idea is central to the theology of Luke-Acts, as Luke tells how the church became a multicultural, multiracial family in Acts 15, 16, and 21. Stories in these three chapters affirm ethnic identity for the two major ethnoracial groups in the early Christian movement and serve as paradigmatic examples for intercultural competency in Christ. While Acts 15 insists that gentiles do not have to become Jews to participate in the new movement, the stories in Acts 16 and 21 likewise ensure that Jews do not have to give up their identity to become like gentiles. Yet, each of them raises questions about the costs of boundary-crossing between tribes.

Intercultural Competency

In antiracist activism, many are beginning to aspire to *intercultural competence*. At one level, the phrase is an update on an older notion of *biculturalism*, which describes someone who can traverse different cultural contexts and be comfortable navigating majority culture and minority culture settings.[6] *Code-switching* is another such phrase that describes this habit among African Americans and others who can put on and take off their cultural mannerisms and speech patterns according to context.[7] Together, these phrases

6. LaFromboise et al., "Psychological Impact of Biculturalism."

7. Chad Nilep offers a more formal definition of code-switching: "Code switching is defined as the practice of selecting or altering linguistic elements so as to contextualize talk in interaction. . . . It may make relevant information beyond the current exchange,

communicate how minorities adapt to different cultural settings because they emerge from and are at home in multiple cultural contexts. Similarly, *third-culture* frameworks include descriptions of "rootlessness" when individuals experience neither identifying with their parents' culture nor the new culture in which they are immersed.[8] So, while biculturals and third-culture individuals can navigate more than one setting, it is possible that these people also experience a comparable pain of not being at home anywhere, of not knowing to whom they belong. I suggest that a similar alienation can apply to the ministry of racial justice allies. This is the pain that might have pushed Rachel Dolezal into pursuing identity fraud.

I think the author of Luke-Acts was a biculturally competent Jew fluent in code-switching, equally at home in Hellenistic Judaism as he was in well-educated Greco-Roman society. He affirmed blended traditions, foods, norms, and languages.[9] He had a masterful command of the Scriptures of Israel on the one hand and a deep familiarity with Greco-Roman culture, literary conventions, and politics on the other. The Gospel of Luke reflects on the significance of Jesus for a mission to the marginalized in Israel, while Acts extends this wide welcome to the Greco-Roman world that they too, might find their Savior in Jesus. In other words, a key metaphor for Luke's vision of the people of God is the blended family of Christian Jews and gentiles, a family negotiating the tension between reverence for traditions alongside an enthusiastic embrace of the new work of Spirit who breaks down barriers and erects new structures. In the account of Pentecost in Acts 2, we see that the ideal family is diverse, encompassing members from all corners of the cosmos.[10] It is intercultural and supernaturally equipped to transcend the boundaries of geography and culture (Acts 2:5–11, 15–21). Acts 5–6 shows that the family of God cares for its own and grows by its ability to transcend conflict. It is a family that prays with one accord and meets its members' material needs. It is composed of Greek- and Aramaic-speaking Jews and God-fearing gentiles; it is a cross-cultural family that must learn to bridge differences and respect boundaries.

---

including knowledge of society and diverse identities" ("Code Switching"). For a light-hearted, charming demonstration of code-switching, see the video at https://youtu.be/lhJ_5Je30EY.

8. For more on third-culture frameworks, see Hanek et al., "Individual Differences."

9. See Gifford Rhamie's account of Luke's cosmopolitan sensibilities, which are influential in my interpretation of the theme of interculturalism in Luke-Acts ("Whiteness, Conviviality and Agency").

10. While the gathering at Pentecost is somewhat homogenous, in that all of the participants are Jews, it is nonetheless true that these Jews were from all countries, representing the horizons of the known world for Jews (Acts 2:5–11).

As we focus on the metaphor of the blended family as Luke's governing paradigm for theological reflection on the early Christian period, we can gain critical leverage from concepts describing movement between cultures. First, in the United States, *assimilation* is a process by which an individual from a minority culture of origin begins to acquire the dominant White culture's beliefs, values, and practices with the hope or expectation that the dominant culture will accept the individual as a bona fide member of that culture.[11] Assimilation can be a crucial survival strategy and contributes to positive life outcomes like higher education levels and family incomes. However, there is stress associated with assimilation, such as discrimination by the majority culture and poor coping behaviors that respond to prejudice. Today, many people think that assimilation is more harmful than healthy.

The opposite process is the process of ethnic identification. Whereas a high level of majority culture involvement is assimilation, a high level of ethnic culture involvement is defined as *ethnic identification*. Ethnic identification involves intentional grounding in and identification with the culture of origin. Importantly, there is a positive relationship between self-esteem and high levels of ethnic identification among African Americans, Latinx, and Whites alike, a result that flies in the face of assimilation as a social ideal. Biculturalism includes a deep knowledge of the cultural beliefs and values in both the culture of origin and the dominant culture, maintaining a positive attitude towards people in both groups. Intercultural competency is similar but goes beyond biculturalism by being grounded in a strong sense of ethnic identification that empowers one to negotiate a second culture successfully. Studies indicate that these individuals exhibit higher cognitive functioning and mental health status than monocultural or assimilated people.

Interculturalism isn't about homogenizing or flattening cultural differences. Neither does it insist on wholesale affirmation of any single culture. Interculturalism involves a posture of openness to cultural differences from within a particular standpoint. It means sharing one's cultural values while eagerly learning from and about others' specific viewpoints. It starts with ethnic identification, with *centering* one's own cultural values even during cultural conflict but doing so without disparaging other choices. Theologically, intercultural competency means recognizing that there is no human culture in which God has not left a witness, a measure of truth, and a touch of God's glory to instruct those with eyes to see.

The author of Acts recognizes that the ability to welcome outsiders is intricately tied to one's ability to bear with internal differences. The degree

11. This discussion of assimilation and biculturalism in Acts draws on my latest book. See chapters 3 and 5 in Sechrest, *Race and Rhyme*.

to which Jews can welcome gentiles into the family of God is connected to the prior capacity for Jews to embrace Jews who are on the fringes. This idea is why Luke begins with the mission to marginalized Jews: the tax collectors and the sinners. Then, in Acts, the gospel goes to the Samaritans outside of Jerusalem, to the Ethiopians from the ends of the earth, and to a rather violent rabbi from the diaspora named Saul, before going to the gentiles in the Roman Empire. Similarly, our inability as Americans to welcome immigrants from beyond our borders is deeply connected to our failure to find common ground with native-born minorities within the American family. This dynamic is the one that links anti-immigrant sentiment to the ongoing problems with race in the United States. It gives rise to the many hues of racism in the USA: racism as anti-Indigenous, anti-Latinx, anti-Asian, and—foundational for many of these—anti-Black.

Now that we have a firmer grasp of how critical theory about race and ethnicity connects with the text, we can look at the three episodes in Acts 15, 16, and 21.

Interculturalism and the Jerusalem Council (Acts 15:1–21)

Functioning as the literary hinge for the grand narrative of Acts, Acts 15 tells how the multiethnic people of God become a blended family in which biculturalism and interculturalism are normative.[12] In the story of the Jerusalem Council, the apostles realize, by reflecting on the work of the Spirit among the gentiles, that gentile Christians do not need to be circumcised for salvation. When church elders reported seeing gentiles speaking in tongues just like the Jews did at Pentecost, they realized that God does not discriminate between ethnic groups.

The action starts in Acts 15:5 with a group of conservative Christian Pharisees. These conservatives insist that the gentiles must be circumcised, with the implication that they must observe all 616 laws in the Torah, because that's what it means to be circumcised, as Paul maintains in Galatians 5:3.[13] Thus, these Christian Pharisees demand that all believers obey all of God's laws. However, note that, in context, *this was a reasonable demand.*[14] They

---

12. I. Howard Marshall describes Acts 15 as the theological and structural centerpiece of Acts (*Acts of the Apostles*, 242).

13. Gal 5:3 NRSV: "Once again I testify to every man who lets himself be circumcised that he is obliged to obey the entire law." Here, Paul's warning shows that many Jews of the period understood that circumcision was a proclamation of an intent to obey the law in its entirety. See also Craig Keener's description of this conservative group in *Acts*, 358.

14. For more on why Jewish Christians would have demanded that gentile Christians

were the faction demanding faithfulness to the laws that had defined the identity of the people of God since the time of Moses. In other words, the liberals are requesting a deviation from hundreds of years of religious history, and this is the group that has the burden of proof. But in verse 7, Peter's eyewitness account of the activity of the Holy Spirit among the gentiles carried the day, showing tongues as a divine sanction of a radical new moment in the life of the church. God is doing a new thing, and God sent the Holy Spirit to communicate that it is time for the people of God to change their ways. Gentiles do not have to become Jews.

The apostolic decree in Acts 15:19–21 gives insight into three principles guiding the mediation between the liberal faction and the traditional conservative faction of the early church. The first principle is that the newcomers should not be harmed (v. 19).[15] The second principle is compromise. This idea is implicit in verse 20, where a small subset of the Mosaic law is imposed on the gentiles: on the one hand the whole law would be burdensome and harmful for gentiles; but on the other hand wholesale elimination of the law would insult Jews.[16] Likewise, the third principle is implicit in verse 21, where the text prioritizes unity. That verse establishes that the presumed context for the new diverse community is the traditional synagogue and not the creation of new worship spaces. Luke longs to expand the family into a single blended unit, without fracturing into disparate segments.

While prioritizing safety for minorities within a majority culture, Luke pragmatically sets out a biculturalism that affirms a degree of assimilation. The elimination of circumcision was a radical gentile-identity-affirming innovation, especially for communities that would continue to meet in synagogues. Yet, equally important, the decree also affirms that Jewish culture would be the dominant culture in the blended family. The biculturalism of the book of Acts combines respect for the Jewish heritage with respect for the new things that God's Holy Spirit was doing among the gentiles.

---

should be circumcised and maintain obedience to the law, see Marshall, *Acts*, 242–43; Keener, *Acts*, 362–63.

15. For more on this theme, see Barrett, *Acts*.

16. Keener, *Acts: An Exegetical Commentary*, 2:2258. A comment from John Calvin in Barrett's commentary is illuminating on this point: "It is not fitting for the ceremonies to be abolished so quickly, as if at one fell swoop, because the Jews had already been accustomed to the teaching of the law for many generations, and Moses had his preachers; that agreement therefore must be gained for a short time until the freedom, procured by Christ, should gradually be more clearly understood. . . . In the early church . . . no doubt there were more . . . certainly [including] Luke who were happy to proceed on (what seemed to be) common-sense lines" (Barrett, *Acts*, 738, citing Calvin, *Institutes of the Christian Religion*).

This passage has a logic that highlights two pearls for intercultural work in race relations today. First, it limits the harm by setting boundaries on assimilation. Though the United States is a nation of immigrants, it is not thereby a hospitable nation. Newcomers face overwhelming obstacles to thriving, especially if you are darker-skinned and get inserted into our racial hierarchies, from Black to White.[17] The text recognizes that newcomers will face hardships in adapting to the new environment. Still, the passage contends that these burdens must be minimized if there is to be a *healthy* blended family. Second, the text privileges compromise. It is critical to realize that the apostolic decree did not ultimately settle the issue. Today, the gentile church does not observe this subset of the Torah. The fact is, no one was happy with the compromise in Acts 15, and there were continuing renegotiations as the arc of church history bent towards living out God's will that the blended family would thrive and grow.

Likewise, there are perils latent in the story, warning against performing the text *in precisely the same way* in today's more complicated racial environment. The most serious difficulty is that the participants develop the compromise without any gentile believers at the table. Today, we know that it is paternalistic to decide what will harm a group without consulting it beforehand. Another obstacle for performing the text is that the Holy Spirit's gift of tongues operated in the early church to give insight about the will of God for the incorporation of gentiles. Yet, it is more difficult to discern when God is doing a new thing without supernatural signs. Or maybe we need eyes to see when supernatural things are happening around us. God, help us to participate with you in the new things you are doing among us!

A Greek-Passing Jew: The Circumcision of Timothy (Acts 16:1–5)

Acts 16:1–5 follows directly on the heels of the Jerusalem Council narrated in Acts 15. Luke places the story of Timothy's circumcision in Acts 16:1–5 shortly after Paul, Barnabas, and Silas take the apostolic decree to the churches in the diaspora. The episode recounting the circumcision of Timothy is a straightforward one but raises a host of questions, the preeminent of which is "Why would Paul circumcise Timothy, given what we just read in Acts 15?"[18] The Jerusalem decree says that gentiles do not have to be circumcised. I suggest that the episode affirms Jewish identity, like the preceding chapter does

17. K. Campbell, "Dry Hate"; Jacobson, *Whiteness of Different Color*; Brodkin, *How Jews Became White.*

18. See the discussion in Keener, *Acts: An Exegetical Commentary*, 2:2320–21.

for gentile identity. But I also think the episode intends to say more about the strength of Paul's ethnic identification than it intends to say about Timothy, who virtually disappears as a significant character in Acts after this episode.

The mention of the cities Derbe and Lystra in Acts 16:1 and the nearby city of Iconium prompts us to reexamine Paul's experiences in those regions.[19] We learn that Paul and Barnabas converted both Jews and Greeks (Acts 14:1) when they started preaching in the synagogue in Iconium. Then they encountered resistance from unbelieving Jews, and these Jews then incited others to stir up the crowds against Paul and Barnabas to the point where the evangelists had to leave the city.[20] Something similar happens in Lystra, the next city the evangelists visit, where Paul miraculously heals a man who had never been able to walk. But just as before, Jewish outsiders from Iconium and elsewhere succeed in turning the crowds against Paul and Barnabas.[21] In other words, unbelieving Jews in Iconium were targeting gentile believers in Iconium and Lystra.

It is against this backdrop that we should evaluate Luke's story about Timothy's circumcision. When Luke tells us that Timothy's father is a Greek, we take that to mean that his father was not a believer.[22] Timothy would certainly have been uncircumcised, following his father's identity, and there is no question that Jews would have made this assumption.[23] So when Paul meets the uncircumcised Timothy in Lystra and learns that Timothy is well-liked by the Christians[24] in nearby Iconium, Paul worries, because he remembers the persecution he faced from the Jews in Iconium. I picture Paul concerned about how the nonbelieving Jews in Iconium would treat Timothy in my sanctified imagination.[25] He knows that non-Christian Jews have targeted gentile believers, and he wants to keep Timothy from harm. Paul circumcised Timothy because he didn't want Timothy to be a target of Jews who were especially hostile to gentile converts.[26] So, Timothy's circumcision was *not* because Paul wanted Timothy to obey the law henceforth. That really would undermine the

19. In the stories preceding this episode in Acts, Derbe seems mostly to be a place of refuge for Paul and his companions as shown in 14:6–7 and 14:19–21.

20. Acts 14:2–7.

21. Acts 14:19–21.

22. Note that all of the those identified as Greeks in Acts are unbelievers. See references to Greeks in Acts 14:1; 16:1, 3; 17:4; 18:4; 19:10, 17; 20:21; and 21:28.

23. Keener, *Acts: An Exegetical Commentary*, 3:2317; also see Keener's discussion of intermarriage, 3:2312–17.

24. I.e., ἀδελφῶν, Acts 16:1–2.

25. For more on this theme, see Gafney's discussion of how the "sanctified imagination" operates in womanist interpretation in *Womanist Midrash*, 6.

26. Acts 16:3–5.

magnificent compromise represented by the apostolic decree that Paul himself was delivering to churches all over the diaspora.[27] Instead, Paul takes preemptive action to protect Timothy from harm, a goal that is in keeping with the logic of the decree.

This passage in Acts 16 has several similarities to the politics of passing. Passing, or passing for White, was a means of protection from harm for those African Americans who had White skin color, hair texture, and facial features. By adopting the manners and customs of Whites, these White-passing African Americans could escape the perils of discrimination, substandard living conditions, and racist violence. They could obtain good jobs and a good education. While passing might be understandable, considering the benefits it offered, some in the minority culture consider it despicable, provoking a rage that might be similar to what the Iconium Jews had for gentiles being welcomed into Jewish synagogues.

Womanist New Testament scholar Mitzi Smith points out that Paul's circumcision of Timothy in Acts 16:1–5 sounds a lot like *respectability politics*, which I think of as a first cousin to passing. According to Smith, respectability politics prevail when people of color adopt White cultural norms and standards of behavior to earn respect and acquire access to White folk's privileges and protections.[28] She argues that Paul performed respectability politics when he compelled Timothy's circumcision, notwithstanding the apostolic decree. Respectability politics is an assimilationist survival technique where racialized people try to earn the right to social worth by "acting White" through conservative dress and behavior. Smith argues that Timothy "earns" his place in Paul's mission by submitting to a rite that was neither demanded by his mixed-race status nor the Jerusalem elders.[29] She concludes that respectability politics leaves the oppressed as somehow "responsible" for the racism they encounter, because they can never be respectable enough.[30]

---

27. Acts 16:4.

28. Smith, "Paul, Timothy, and the Respectability Politics of Race."

29. "Paul had the authority and influence to place the burden of circumcision on Timothy, despite the Jerusalem Council's decree, and he did. Paul's bias and fears superseded the just decision of the Council not to place the burden of circumcision on the Gentiles. . . . We might argue that Paul is a good person. He has sacrificed his well-being to take the gospel to the Gentiles; he meant no harm. But he still operates from a position of racial bias and as the one with the authority and power, his bias is oppressive, harmful, consequential, and impacts Timothy's quality of life. Sometimes white people know that the pound of flesh that other white people demand of non-white bodies is unjust and overly burdensome, but they are silent and thus complicit in racism" (Smith, "Paul, Timothy, and the Respectability Politics of Race").

30. Smith, "Paul, Timothy, and the Respectability Politics of Race," citing Whitney Alese, "Seven Reasons Why Respectability Politics Are BS."

Yet another way of reading this story is to see it as a narrative about Timothy's Greek-passing life. As part Greek, Timothy was able to pass as a member of the dominant group in that society, with access to rank, resources, and valuable relationships. Because Jewish identity was a marginalized identity in the Roman Empire, more social benefits were available to Timothy as a Greek than as a Jew. While he was uncircumcised and passing as Greek, Timothy could hope to advance socially in the gymnasium, the center of education for Greek males, where they often trained in the nude. The decree tells us that gentiles don't have to be circumcised, but it doesn't say anything about Jews who try to cover up their circumcision and pass as Greek, as some of them did when they wanted social mobility. So, while Paul is trying to protect Timothy from harm, he is also figuratively telling Timothy, "Keep your locks! Don't get them shaved off!" Circumcision was a physical feature that defined ethnic identity, and Paul insists that this biracial Jew honor his stigmatized Jewish half.

Moral reflection on this episode is complex, given the emotionally charged topic among minoritized communities. Minoritized people who can pass for White do it to gain advantages for themselves. Still, they do it at the cost of either severing or harming contact with their families and communities of origin.[31] I know of a White-passing Black woman in the Jim Crow 1930s who placed her darker-skinned child in an orphanage while she dated a White man, in hopes of marrying him. Against pain like that, I see Timothy's circumcision as an act of ethnic identification in the context of a partial, though stigmatized, identity. And as someone with a stigmatized Black female identity, I can't help but see this as an act of nobility, one that conveys emotional and mental health advantages as well.

On the other hand there are *perils* in this story of ethnic identification, which can be problematic as concerns hybrid identities. We've already talked about respectability politics, which are so damaging to communities of color. But another legacy of slavery is how slaveowners produced more slaves by breeding and raping Black women and consigning their mixed-race offspring to slavery. These Blacks were consigned to an inferior caste because they had more than just one drop of African blood—called the one-drop rule. Today, one could argue about whether Timothy received a higher or lower status after the circumcision in the narrative context, but what is problematic is that there has to be the assignment at all. The fact that we are policing the barrier of mixed-race identity and forcing someone to choose one part of their identity

---

31. For an evocative exposition of these themes, see Rebecca Hall's 2021 film *Passing*, based on the novel by Nella Larsen.

and erase the other means leaving racist ideologies about racial belonging intact.

Ever a True Jew: Paul and the Jerusalem Church (Acts 21:17–40)

In our third and last passage, we find Paul traveling to Rome by way of Jerusalem after spending over two years in Ephesus. All along the route to Jerusalem, there are indications that he is heading into dangerous territory. Nonetheless, he receives a warm welcome from fellow believers when he lands in the city.[32] His difficulties do not start until the following day, when he visits James and the church elders after talking about his ministry success among the gentiles.[33]

From a literary perspective, it turns out that this episode in Acts 21 is similar to the one about the Jerusalem Council in Acts 15.[34] Both passages show Paul receiving a warm welcome from the church and elders.[35] Both episodes begin with Paul giving a recap of how God has worked through Paul's ministry among the gentiles.[36] Both cases focus on the relationship between the community and the Jewish law.[37] In both cases, Paul's key opponents are Jewish believers who are zealous for the law.[38] However, while this zealousness was negatively associated with Christian Pharisees in Acts 15, in Acts 21, being "zealous for the law" is now a positive characteristic associated with the elders. Indeed, Paul himself is depicted as being zealous for the law in this passage. Thus, these texts differ in one fundamental respect: in Acts 21, the claim is that Jews are being told to *abandon* circumcision and the law (21:21), while Acts 15 is about telling gentiles to *observe* circumcision and the law (15:4). This difference is our first indication that Acts 15 is about gentile identity, while this chapter centers on Jewish identity.

James reports that law-observant Jewish believers have been told that Paul has abandoned his Jewish heritage and teaches others to do the same. Later, in verses 27 to 29, a second accusation says he violated the sanctity of the temple by bringing a gentile into it, probably referring to one of the temple

---

32. Acts 21:3–4, 11–13; cf. Acts 19:21; 20:22–23.

33. Acts 21:17–19.

34. Thompson, "Say It Ain't so," 38–39.

35. Acts 21:17–18; 15:4.

36. Acts 21:19; 15:4.

37. Acts 21:20–21; 15:1.

38. Acts 21:20; 15:5.

precincts closed to gentiles. The underlying question is whether Paul's work among the gentiles has compromised his loyalty to his own people.

The elders of the Jerusalem church advise Paul to prove his loyalty by taking vows requiring substantial temple sacrifices *and* paying for the offerings associated with the vows of four others. Many scholars think that the vows in question are Nazirite vows, requiring substantial sacrificial offerings at vow completion.[39] According to Num 6:14–15, these sacrifices included two young lambs, a ram, a basket of unleavened bread, and flour cakes. These requirements remained,[40] notwithstanding the capacity of the Nazirite to pay.[41] Therefore, a scheme that required Paul to pay for Nazirite vows for five would have required sacrificing fifteen animals or the equivalent of two herds.[42] So, when James asks Paul to demonstrate his loyalty to the law this way, he has given him a task that only the most dedicated and scrupulous person would do. Paul readily agrees to a proposal that goes far beyond the call of duty and communicates to all onlookers that he is indeed a faithful Jew, zealous for the law.[43]

The expense of paying for these vows was so large that some have wondered how Paul found the funds for the undertaking.[44] It turns out that the answer may be in Paul's Epistles. When he came to Jerusalem for the last time, he brought a gift of money collected from gentile churches in the diaspora for the poor in the Jerusalem church.[45] If this is the case, then the Jerusalem church, in effect, tells Paul that they would rather see him use the collection to prove his loyalty and establish his Jewish identity beyond a shadow of doubt than to receive poverty relief money as an offering from the gentiles.[46] This

39. Marshall, *Acts*, 345; Bruce, *Book of Acts*, 430ff; cf. Barrett, *Acts*, 1010, who acknowledges the similarities to those vows but notes difficulties with whether the story comports in all details with Nazirite vows.

40. Marshall, *Acts*, 343–44.

41. Num 6:21.

42. A flock typically had about seven animals in each group; see Lewis and Llewellyn-Jones, *Culture of Animals*, 84.

43. In this essay, I am less interested in questions about the historicity of Paul's actions as narrated by Luke than I am about Luke's theological agenda regarding intercultural competence. Readers who want to reconcile Paul's participation in the Nazirite vows with his sentiments in 1 Cor 9:19–23 should consult the discussion in Barrett, *Acts*, 1013.

44. Barrett, *Acts*, 1011.

45. 1 Cor 16:1–2; 2 Cor 8:1–4; Rom 15:25; cf. Gal 2:10; Acts 24:17. Barrett suggests that delivering the offering from gentile churches was likely the historical reason for Paul's visit to Jerusalem on this occasion (*Acts*, 1001).

46. Though we cannot know for sure that the Jerusalem church asked Paul to use the collection in the way imagined, it is not hard to imagine their reticence to receive the monies that might have put them in a patronage-client relationship with the gentile

scene shows that ethnic identification can mean as much to the community as it does to the individual.

Were the charges of disloyalty false? From the perspective of Acts, we would have to say that they are mistaken.[47] Luke has given us many indications that Paul was a loyal Jew: his initial zeal against Stephen and the nascent church early in Acts; his interest in Timothy's circumcision *after* the Jerusalem compromise; his willingness to take on Nazirite vows; and his enthusiasm in underwriting these expensive vows for four others as well. Several times in the narrative, Paul describes himself as a Hebrew-speaking Pharisee, a sect known for their conscientious and meticulous observance of the law. His ability to speak the ancestral language calms a murderous crowd, angered at rumors of his disloyalty (Acts 22:2). Paul emerges as thoroughly invested in his ethnic identification as a Jew in all these cases.[48]

Yet, this episode highlights the potential costs of interculturalism. Though Luke was convinced that Paul was a faithful Jew, despite accusations of infidelity to the Mosaic law, it is clear that Paul's identity was compromised among other Jews because of his work among gentiles. His own people become very suspicious about whether he identified with them. Tragically, Paul does "lose" his identity in the episode, because no one believes him. He is never quite able to regain the confidence of his kinfolk because of his work with the ethnic other. Paul has become a "race-traitor."

This phrase has an ugly history. White supremacists and bigots have used similar language and acts of racialized terrorism to frighten White allies from keeping their antiracist commitments. Like Paul, allies for social justice who spend their lives on behalf of the marginalized can be ridiculed by members of their own communities for aligning themselves with the ethnic other. Accusations about a lack of loyalty and the subsequent fractures in the community are deeply painful. *I would suggest that ethnic identification can help activists survive and thrive while keeping a firm grip on their identity in Christ.* Even as the riot was unfolding around him, Paul responded by telling his story. He spoke of his people, his errors, his transformation, his work, and his

---

churches in the diaspora. For an in-depth consideration of the theological significance of the collection in Paul, see Downs, *Offering of the Gentiles.*

47. Marshall, *Acts*, 344; Barrett, *Acts*, 1007–9.

48. Some readers might be confused by my conclusion here about Paul's investment in his Jewish identity, given the title of my first book, *A Former Jew: Paul and the Dialectics of Race.* Though space does not permit a fuller answer here, a short response to this tension is that I maintain that Paul and Luke, while both Jewish, had differing postures about the salience of ethnic identity in Christ. Whereas Luke favored an intercultural fluidity and dexterity as described here, Paul's solution involved a situationally selective hierarchical ordering of overlapping identities (cf. 1 Cor 9:19–23; Gal 3:28).

confidence as a follower of Christ. Ethnic identification is a crucial resource for being grounded in long-term work among the ethnic other.

But the background and details of this story show that the kind of intercultural competence that Paul exhibited in work among gentiles didn't actually threaten his Jewish identity. When you remember that Paul had a minoritized identity in the Roman Empire, his actions in these three episodes underline the positive affirmation of his minority identity. He traveled across the diaspora to encourage gentile adoption of a subset of Jewish traditions. He promoted Timothy's Jewish identity, even though Timothy had been happily passing as Greek in the majority culture. And he willingly took on the vows of a Nazirite for five people at a high cost. His Jewish identity was as strong as ever, despite his work as the apostle to the gentiles.

CONCLUSION: ETHNIC IDENTIFICATION AND INTERCULTURALISM

In conclusion, Acts 15, 16, and 21 give us three fundamental values about the faith:

1) The church must be inclusive, welcoming others (gentiles) into a blended family that balances the old and the new.

2) (Gentile) participation in the people of God does not demand wholesale assimilation into the dominant (Jewish) culture.

3) Welcoming others (gentiles) into the family of God does not threaten or diminish the dominant culture's (Jewish) identity.

In Luke's theological vision of community, interculturalism goes hand in hand with ethnic identification. God affirms ethnic identification in Acts on both sides of the blended family. Ethnicity is a strength and a gift, not a problem to be overcome. Acts also teaches that the strength derived from ethnic identification can and should be combined with an intercultural openness to cultural difference, whether in crossing back and forth between your home culture and a new one or engaging many different cultural spheres like Paul did. You can and should appreciate elements in all cultures while still being true to your own heritage and culture. This rootedness will give you strength in challenging times. It will ground you in God's creative gift of designing you just so, placing you just so, and anointing you for work in specific places.

In these stories, Paul is a paradigmatic example of intercultural competence. He is the marginalized person who knew who he was and encouraged others to find their way to an authentic, inclusive, gospel-centered identity that honors God's sovereign work of placing persons in a particular place and people group. Paul is also an example of the social justice ally who speaks up for the marginalized *among his own people*. He counted the cost but kept on giving, and he never lost his sense of who he was. He told his story and was faithful to his mission to bring in the gentile other until the end. Though we look to Paul as an example, we will be more careful than he was. We will not try to speak for the other in their absence. We will speak on their behalf when we are alone among our own people, seeking to increase their readiness to accept and love the other in Christ. But we will not dishonor God's creative choice in placing us in a specific narrative by appropriating different peoples' stories as our own.

Modern Christians need to be adept at crossing cultural boundaries for the sake of our Christian witness. Like the author of Luke-Acts, we need to have a masterful command of Scriptures, knowing how it continues to speak on the matter of ethnoracial inclusion. Also, like the author of Luke-Acts, we need to have a deep familiarity with our racialized culture, history, and politics. We need deep engagement with the stories of as many of the multiethnic peoples in the US as possible. Others may be confused about whose people we are and where our loyalties lie—even our own people. But we know *who* we are and *whose* we are. We know that we belong to a people whose members come from every single last tribe and race under heaven. And, God help us, we will not turn our backs on that calling.

BIBLIOGRAPHY

Andone, Dakin. "A Varsity Wrestler Was Told to Cut His Dreadlocks or Forfeit the Match. Now the Attorney General Is Investigating." *CNN*, 22 Dec 2018. https://edition.cnn.com/2018/12/22/us/wrestler-dreadlocks-new-jersey-investigation/index.html.

Barrett, C. K. *The Acts of the Apostles*. International Critical Commentary 2. Edinburgh: T. & T. Clark, 1998.

Brodkin, Karen. *How Jews Became White Folks and What That Says about Race in America*. New Brunswick, NJ: Rutgers University Press, 1999.

Bruce, F. F. *The Book of Acts*. New International Commentary on the New Testament. Grand Rapids: Eerdmans, 1988.

Campbell, Alexia Fernández. "A Black Woman Lost a Job Offer Because She Wouldn't Cut Her Dreadlocks. Now She Wants to Go to the Supreme Court." *Vox*, 18 Apr 2018. https://www.vox.com/2018/4/18/17242788/chastity-jones-dreadlock-job-discrimination.

Campbell, Kristina M. "A Dry Hate: White Supremacy and Anti-Immigrant Rhetoric in the Humanitarian Crisis on the U.S.-Mexico Border." *West Virginia Law Review* 1081 (Spring 2015) 1082–1130.

Downs, David J. *The Offering of the Gentiles: Paul's Collection for Jerusalem in Its Chronological, Cultural, and Cultic Contexts*. 2008. Reprint, Grand Rapids: Eerdmans, 2016.

Gafney, Wilda. *Womanist Midrash: A Reintroduction to the Women of the Torah and the Throne*. Louisville: Westminster John Knox, 2017.

Griffin, Chanté. "How Natural Black Hair at Work Became a Civil Rights Issue." *JSTOR Daily*, 3 July 2019. https://daily.jstor.org/how-natural-black-hair-at-work-became-a-civil-rights-issue/.

Hall, Rebecca, dir. *Passing*. New York: AUM, 2021.

Hanek, Kathrin J., et al. "Individual Differences among Global/Multicultural Individuals: Cultural Experiences, Identity, and Adaptation." *International Studies of Management & Organization* 44 (2014) 75–89.

Jacobson, Matthew Frye. *Whiteness of a Different Color: European Immigrants and the Alchemy of Race*. Cambridge, MA: Harvard University Press, 1999.

Keener, Craig. *Acts*. New Cambridge Bible Commentary. Cambridge: Cambridge University Press, 2020.

———. *Acts: An Exegetical Commentary*. 3 vols. Grand Rapids: Baker Academic, 2014.

LaFromboise, Teresa, et al. "Psychological Impact of Biculturalism: Evidence and Theory." *Psychological Bulletin* 114 (1993) 395–412.

Lewis, Sian, and Lloyd Llewellyn-Jones. *The Culture of Animals in Antiquity: A Sourcebook with Commentaries*. New York: Routledge, 2018.

Marshall, I. Howard. *The Acts of the Apostles*. Tyndale New Testament Commentaries. Grand Rapids: Eerdmans, 1980.

Nguyễn, Ann Thúy, and Maya Pendleton. "Recognizing Race in Language: Why We Capitalize 'Black' and 'White.'" *Center for the Study of Social Policy*, 23 Mar 2020. https://cssp.org/2020/03/recognizing-race-in-language-why-we-capitalize-black-and-white/.

Nilep, Chad. "'Code Switching' in Sociocultural Linguistics." *Colorado Research in Linguistics* 19 (2006). https://doi.org/10.25810/hnq4-jv62.

Oluo, Ijeoma. "The Heart of Whiteness: Ijeoma Oluo Interviews Rachel Dolezal, the White Woman Who Identifies as Black." *The Stranger*, 19 Apr 2017. https://www.thestranger.com/features/2017/04/19/25082450/the-heart-of-whiteness-ijeoma-oluo-interviews-rachel-dolezal-the-white-woman-who-identifies-as-black.

Rhamie, Gifford. "Whiteness, Conviviality and Agency: The Ethiopian Eunuch (Acts 8:26–40) and Conceptuality in the Imperial Imagination of Biblical Studies." PhD diss., Canterbury Christ Church University, 2019.

Sechrest, Love Lazarus. *A Former Jew: Paul and the Dialectics of Race*. London: T. & T. Clark, 2009.

———. *Race and Rhyme: Rereading the New Testament*. Grand Rapids: Eerdmans, 2022.

Singer, Reid. "What Andrew Johnson Endured Shines a Light on Amateur Wrestling's Institutional Failures." *SBNation*, 28 Dec 2018. https://www.sbnation.com/2018/12/28/18159127/andrew-johnson-amateur-wrestling-dreadlocks-institutional-failures.

Smith, Mitzi J. "Paul, Timothy, and the Respectability Politics of Race: A Womanist Inter(con)textual Reading of Acts 16:1–5." *Religions* 10.3 (2019) 190. https://doi.org/10.3390/rel10030190.

St. Félix, Doreen. "'The Rachel Divide' Review: A Disturbing Portrait of Dolezal's Racial Fraudulence." *The New Yorker*, 26 Apr 2018. https://www.newyorker.com/culture/

culture-desk/the-rachel-divide-review-a-disturbing-portrait-of-dolezals-racial-fraudulence.

Thompson, Richard P. "'Say It Ain't so, Paul!' The Accusations Against Paul in Acts 21 in Light of His Ministry in Acts 16–20." *Biblical Research* 45 (2000) 34–50.

Young, Sarah. "Gabrielle Union Shares Photos of Hairstyles That Were 'Too Black' for *America's Got Talent*." *Independent*, 14 Dec 2019. https://www.independent.co.uk/life-style/gabrielle-union-hairstyles-video-instagram-americas-got-talent-racism-a9246856.html.

2

Reframing a Component of Creation Theology

The Imago Dei as the Baseline for Confronting Racial Injustice

WINFRED OMAR NEELY

INTRODUCTION

THE TRIUNE GOD IS the Creator of the universe (Gen 1:1, 2:4; Ps 8:3, 33:6; John 1:1–3). To this moment, the triune God sustains the universe that he brought into existence out of nothing (Col 1:17; Heb 1:3). If the Lord ceased for one second to exercise his sustaining power on our behalf, all of us and the entire universe would immediately descend into nothingness. Since we depend on God utterly for the maintenance of our very existence, all our problems are theological in nature, and the solutions to these problems are of necessity theological. Racial and ethnic injustices are theological problems, and their solutions must be theological in nature.

Thus, in confronting the empirical realities of racial and ethnic injustice in our world, we must lay the biblical and theological foundation for the rationale to confront these virulent manifestations of sin. Of course, 200 years before the advent of critical theory and critical race theory, some African American readers of Scripture such as Jupiter Hammon, Lemuel Haynes,

Jarena Lee, and David Walker provided the biblical and theological foundation to confront these sins,[1] but these interpreters were marginalized because of their black bodies, and their prophetic voices were unheeded.

Given that beginnings still matter (Gen 1:1; Matt 19:3–6; John 1:1; 1 John 1:1; 2:7, 14), I will go back to the beginning and will reframe[2] the component of creation theology that deals with the image of God. In reframing the theological reality of the image of God, this paper will argue that the *imago Dei* is the starting point and theological ground for confronting racial and ethnic injustice in all of its manifestations in our world today.

THE *IMAGO DEI*

The question that guides our analysis is "What is a human being?" In answering this question, I will focus on the image of God. I will also use some linguistic insights from cognitive grammar to understand and nuance the semantic significance of the expression "the image of God."

Genesis 1:26 reads:

> And God said, let us make Adam in our *image*, according to our likeness, and let them rule over the fish of the sea and over the birds of the heavens, and over the cattle, and over all the earth and over all creatures that creep over the earth. And God created the Adam in his *image*, in the *image* of God created he him, male and female he created them (author's translation).

Before the analysis of verse 26, note some of the preceding commandments in Genesis 1:

- "Let there be light" (v. 3).

- "Let there be an expanse in the midst of the waters" (v. 6).

- "Let the waters under the heavens be gathered together in one place" (v. 9).

- "Let there be lights in the expanse of the heavens" (v. 14).

- "Let the earth bring forth living creatures according to their kind" (v. 24).

---

1. Bowens, *African American Readings*, 15–112.

2. The study of the image of God in this paper occurs within the framework of cognitive grammar, a theoretical linguistic framework developed by Ronald Langacker. See Langacker, *Essentials of Cognitive Grammar*, 1–89. As far as I know, this paper is the first attempt to study the concept of the image of God within the theoretical framework of cognitive grammar.

Now notice the shift in the language of verse 26: "Then God said, 'Let us make.'" Of all of God's creative acts in the first chapter of Genesis, verse 26 is unique, prefaced with Godhead deliberation. The creation of humanity is unique and special. We concur with Hamilton's observation:

> The shift from the consistent use of the verb in the jussive (e.g., "Let there be") to a cohortative ("Let us make") is enough to prepare the reader for something momentous on this sixth day. That momentous element is the creation of man *in our image, as our likeness.*[3]

The Hebrew word translated by "man" in our English versions is אָדָם, transliterated as *Adam*. The English words man, humanity, or humankind are insufficient as translations of the Hebrew Adam when it refers to humanity. These terms are not specific enough and do not represent the fine-grained semantic resolution and nuance of this usage of the Hebrew Adam. In English, the rendering that has the most communicative significance of this usage of Adam is "earthling" or "earth person."[4]

In cognitive grammar, a noun like Adam in the earthling or earth person sense is a relational noun. Inherent in the meaning of a relational noun is its relationship to another entity. Even though that relationship is not expressed, that relationship is intrinsic to the meaning of a relational noun.[5] Adam means earthling or earth person and is related to אֲדָמָה, transliterated *Adamah*. Adamah is the ground, the reddish brown soil of the earth, the earth stuff Yahweh used to create Adam. "And the Yahweh God formed the Adam, dust from the Adamah, and breathed into his nostrils the breath of life, and the Adam became a living soul" (Gen 2:7, author's translation). The dust of the Adamah does not mean here that God made man from the dust of the ground; instead, the expression "dust from the Adamah" stands in apposition to Adam, describing Adam's essence before he became a living soul. He was dust from the ground (Gen 3:19; 18:27; Ps 103:14). Yahweh forms the dust of the Adamah and breathes life into the formed dust of the ground, and the Adam becomes a living soul.

In deliberation with himself, God creates Adam, the earth person, in his own image. The creation of Adam in the image of God is the central reality and defining element in human identity. Still, the question must be asked: What does it mean to be created in God's image?

---

3. Hamilton, *Book of Genesis*, 134; emphasis in original.
4. Hamilton, "Adam."
5. Van Wolde, *Reframing Biblical Studies*, 112.

We are aware of the different interpretations of the image of God. These various interpretations have massive implications, but space will not permit an exploration into the different ways the *imago Dei* has been interpreted. Nevertheless, the following is a brief sampling of some of the interpretive stances:

1) The image of God means people have a creative capacity like God.

2) The image of God means human beings represent God in his reign over creation.

3) The image of God means that human beings are social beings and have the capacity for fellowship with God and other people.

4) Since God is spirit, the image must be restricted to some spiritual and immaterial aspect of humanity: reason, conscience, soul, spirit, etc.

The narrator of Genesis 1, however, makes no such assertions. The narrator does not restrict the scope of the image or reduce the image to the quest for permanence and the longing for immortality or limit it to functional aspects like reason, the use of the imagination, and the capacity for relationship.

Moreover, in cognitive grammar, a Hebrew noun like צֶלֶם (image) is a relational noun. As a relational noun, its relationship to another entity is an inherent part of its semantic makeup. The noun צֶלֶם (image) profiles a three-dimensional, carved-out, stand-alone figure, "a statue in the round."[6] Additionally, the representation of something else is an inherent part of its semantic base. Thus, צֶלֶם (image) is a three-dimensional, carved-out figure that represents something else.

This brief cognitive analysis of צֶלֶם (image) clarifies what it means for Adam to be created in God's image and places the exegetical conclusion on a firmer linguistic footing. Adam "in the round" is a unified person, a psychosomatic unity created in God's image. The image of God means that Adams—earth persons in their embodiment, in their psychosomatic unity—are representations of God. The image of God is not merely functional or relational; it is something that a human being is in his or her totality.[7] Kidner sums this up well:

> The Bible makes man a unity: acting, thinking, and feeling with his whole being. This living creature, then, and not some distillation from him, is an *expression* or *transcription* of the

6. Waltke, *Genesis*, 65.
7. Erickson, *Christian Theology*, 470.

eternal, incorporeal creator in terms of temporal, bodily, creaturely existence.[8]

Creating Adam in his image, God crowns the earth person with stunning dignity, value, and worth. The juxtaposition of Adam with the image of God is stunning, breathtaking.

It is interesting to note that in the Greek translation of the Old Testament, the Hebrew word צֶלֶם (image) is translated by the Greek word εἰκών, transliterated *icon*. On the home screen of my iPhone are a number of icons, small images that represent and point to different apps or functions. People represent and point to God. Thus, every human being is *iconic*. The Bible conceptualizes human beings in the highest way possible.

Adam is created according to the likeness of God. Image and likeness are related terms, but they are not synonymous, because "in the strict sense, true synonyms at the level of semantic significance do not exist."[9] We are not God, but we are created according to the likeness of God. God is the eternal original after which human beings are patterned. This reality gives ultimate significance to all human life.

AFTER THE FALL

Since Genesis 1 and 2 deal with humanity before the fall, is the image of God something that people are after the fall? Due to space restrictions, we will not consider other views but will simply answer the question in the affirmative. In Gen 5:1, the beginning of the third major division of the book of Genesis, the narrator reminds readers of God's creation of Adam "in the likeness of God" in Genesis 1 and 2. Then Adam fathers a son in his own likeness and image. Since Adam was created in the image of God, even though fallen, that divine image and likeness are passed on to the next generation through the process of procreation (Gen 5:1–3). According to Gen 9:6, human life, though fallen, is still sacred, because people are still image-bearers. In a discussion about the tongue as an instrument on one hand to bless God and at the same time to curse people, echoing Genesis 1 and alluding to Gen 1:26, James writes:

> The tongue is set among our members as that which defiles the entire body, and sets on fire the course of our life, and is set on fire by hell. For every species of beasts and birds, of reptiles and creatures of the sea, is tamed and has been tamed by the human race. But no one can tame the tongue; it is a restless evil and full of

8. Kidner, *Genesis*, 51 (italics added).

9. Neely, "Reframing 2 Samuel," 247.

deadly poison. With it we bless our Lord and Father, and with it we curse men, who have been made in the likeness of God; from the same mouth come both blessing and cursing. My brethren, these things ought not to be this way (Jas 3:6–10 NASB).

The highest use of the tongue is to bless and praise God, but to use the same instrument to curse people is sinful because people are made in the likeness of God. The words "in the likeness of God" are literally "according to the likeness of God" and are the exact language used in Gen 1:26, "according to our likeness," in the Greek translation of the Old Testament. Furthermore, the tense of the Greek participle γεγονότας (have been made) is important here. Who "have been made" is a perfect active plural participle. The perfect tense means that God's act of making was completed in the past (Gen 1:26), and the results of that creative action continue to this day. The results of the creative act of God in creating human beings in his image and according to his likeness continue and are in force today. The participle is plural. All people have been created in the likeness of God. Even though the word image is not mentioned here, it is overheard, because the allusion to Gen 1:26 is a call for readers to dialogue vigorously with Genesis 1. Human beings are still divine image-bearers after the fall. Even though marred, the image is still intact. In short, the image of God in which people were created in Genesis 1 is still in force today. Therefore, the image of God is still the starting point and theological ground for how we view and treat all people today. Grudem encourages us to remember this great fact of human identity:

> Yet we must remember that even fallen, sinful man has the status of being in God's image. Every single human being, no matter how much the image is marred by sin, or illness, or weakness, or age, or any other disability, still has the status of being in God's image and therefore must be treated with dignity and respect that is due to God's image bearer. This has profound implications for our conduct toward others.[10]

PROFOUND IMPLICATIONS

First, as divine image-bearers, all human beings have inherent dignity and infinite worth and value. Human dignity and value are not endowments humans bestow on other humans. Instead, we recognize and affirm the inherent dignity, worth, and value that people already have because they are divine image-bearers and represent God. Due to the great dignity inherent in every

10. Grudem, *Systematic Theology*, 450.

human being, it is our Christian duty and responsibility to treat every human being with respect, to take every life seriously, and to "honor all people" (1 Pet 2:17).

Second, a part of the formation of Christians must involve the cultivation of not only a high view of God and a high view of Scripture but also a high view of people and a deep love and appreciation for the human family in all its ethnic diversity and image-bearing importance. Such spiritual formation is consonant with God's love for all people and the appeal of the gospel to human agency. The call to come to Christ, to believe in Christ, to walk with God are expressions of God's own appreciation for the dignity that he bestowed on his human creatures.

Third, since all people in their psychosomatic unity still represent God, the embodiment of people matters. The different shapes of the human body, the various textures of the hair, the different color of the eyes, the various shades and colors of the skin, and all "we the people" are in our diverse embodiments represent God. Therefore, no particular hair texture or human body shape or skin color is privileged: all equally represent God. Consequently, a scale of value associated with skin color does not exist in God's economy. The human imposition and conceptualization of a scale of color on divine image-bearers, with the color white at the top and black at the bottom, is an egregious and diseased expression of the fallen human mind and is fundamentally an insult to God. We must strenuously resist any notion or efforts that seek to privilege one skin color at the expense of another. All should be celebrated and privileged equally!

Fourth, as salt and light in the world (Matt 5:13–16), Christians are called by the Lord to be redemptive agents of the reformation of systems and structures in order to promote the flourishing of all human beings—even unsaved people—as divine image-bearers (Gal 6:10).

We may need to remind ourselves at this point that due to the sin of Adam and Eve (Gen 3:14–24), the entire universe is fallen and alienated from God (Rom 8:18–21; Col 1:15–20). We live in a fallen world marked by death, mourning, crying, and pain that will not be removed until the creation of the new heavens and the new earth (Rev 21:1–4). Sinful and fallen people who live under the power of sin as a ruling power inhabit our fallen world (Rom 3:9–18). Consequently, all human structures—social, cultural, and governmental—are fallen structures. Even our best systems and governmental structures bear the taint of sin, because fallen people established them. All fallen structures stand in need of assessment, evaluation, and reform. It is idolatrous to think that any system or structure that we set up in this life is beyond the need of repair and reformation. The practical conclusion is this: in the power of the Spirit, based on the gospel, Christians should be healing agents of redemption in our broken world (Matt 5:13–14), leading men and women to Christ and working to bring reformation and healing in every area of life, including the ongoing reformation and healing of fallen structural systems. We embrace a world-formative Christianity[11] and take Christ-centered and biblically informed responsibility for our world and its continual reformation. Wolterstorff observes:

> The saints are responsible for the structure of the social world in which they find themselves. That structure is not simply part of nature; to the contrary, it is the result of human decision, and by concerted effort it can be altered. Indeed, it should be altered, for it is a fallen structure, in need of reform. The responsibility of the saints to struggle for reform of the social order in which they find themselves is one facet of the discipleship to which their Lord Jesus Christ has called them. It is not an addition to their religion; it is there among the very notion of Christian spirituality.[12]

In our struggle for the redemptive transformation of our immediate spheres of influence and our fallen world in general, it is imperative that the church come together as one as we meet a turbulent twenty-first-century world of changing demographics with increasing waves of racial and ethnic tensions. As Yamada has noted:

> Demographers believe that by the year 2040, or somewhere in the middle decades of the twenty-first century, the United States will have no single racial-ethnic majority. This does not mean that racial prejudice or institutional racism will cease to exist. In fact, if the past decade is any indication, racial tensions and social unrest around the issue of race, especially in the United States, will continue to increase.[13]

If, however, the church pivots and truly embraces the *imago Dei* as the starting point and foundation for confronting racial injustice in all its forms today, perhaps the Lord will revive us again and through us work in society in a way that ushers in spiritual, structural, societal, and cultural change. In doing this, we may move closer to the realization of our Lord's request, when he prayed:

---

11. I am indebted to Nicholas Wolterstorff for the concept of world-formative Christianity. See Wolterstorff, *Until Justice and Peace*, 3.

12. Wolterstorff, *Until Justice and Peace*, 3.

13. Yamada, "Living and Teaching," 31.

> I do not ask on behalf of these alone, but for those also who believe in me through their word; that they may all be one; even as you, Father, are in me and I in you, that they also may be in us so that the world may believe that you sent me. (John 17:20–21 NASB)

BIBLIOGRAPHY

Bowens, Lisa M. *African American Readings of Paul: Reception, Resistance & Transformation*. Grand Rapids: Eerdmans, 2020.

Du Bois, W. E. B. *The Souls of Black Folk*. Monee, IL: Millennium, 1903.

Erickson, Millard J. *Christian Theology*. 2nd ed. Grand Rapids: Baker Academic, 2013.

Grudem, Wayne. *Systematic Theology*. Grand Rapids: Zondervan, 1994.

Hamilton, Victor P. "Adam." In *The New International Dictionary of Old Testament Theology and Exegesis*, edited by Willem A. VanGemeren, 1:262–66. 5 vols. Grand Rapids: Zondervan, 1997.

———. *The Book of Genesis: Chapters 1–17*. NICOT. Grand Rapids: Eerdmans, 1990.

Kidner, Derek. *Genesis*. TOTC. Downers Grove, IL: InterVarsity, 1967.

Langacker, Ronald W. *Essentials of Cognitive Grammar*. Oxford: Oxford University Press, 2013.

Neely, Winfred Omar. "Reframing 2 Samuel 11 and 12: An Exercise in Cognitive Hermeneutics and Intertextual Close Reading." PhD diss., University of Aberdeen, 2021.

Van Wolde, Ellen. *Reframing Biblical Studies*. Winona Lake, IN: Eisenbrauns, 2009.

Waltke, Bruce K. *Genesis*. Grand Rapids: Zondervan, 2001

Wolterstorff, Nicholas. *Until Justice and Peace Embrace*. Grand Rapids: Eerdmans, 1983.

Yamada, Frank. "Living and Teaching When Change Is the New Normal: Trends in Theological Education and the Impact on Teaching and Learning." *Wabash Center Journal on Teaching* 1 (Jan 2020) 23–36.

3

The Dividing Wall

Socially Located Exegesis in a Time of Reckoning

Amy Peeler and Madison N. Pierce

Transitions in life are often motivated by both a push and a pull, reasons that both compel *from* a certain way of life as well as aspects that woo *toward* a new one. Neither of us has changed careers or locations in the last few years, but this chapter includes stories of changes in how we think about and act on issues related to race. We explore what it looks like to incorporate our social locations consciously as we read Scripture. We are professors of New Testament, writers in the guild, and active participants in our churches. We draw from experiences in those roles to demonstrate these changes. It has been the push of Scripture and the pull of ecclesial life that have compelled us to make what are, we hope, some life-long changes in the ways we love our neighbors.

Amy Peeler

I am racialized white, which is to say, I have been included in the category "white" as constructed by our society. I am Scottish and English on both sides of my family—or at least that is the narrative I've been told and have accepted. I'm sure the reality is more complicated. This fact is pertinent because, as a result of my racialization, I have had the privilege of contemplating issues of race very little before 2020.

Before the exegesis of the biblical text that provides the clarion call for right living between *racial* or *ethnic* people groups, those terms demand explanation. It has become common to distinguish race, which focuses on physical characteristics, from that of ethnicity, which focuses on culture, but both "convey a sense of peoplehood based on shared descent."[1] Advances in this field of research illuminate how fluid rather than fixed these categories really are. Not only is one's ancestry rarely as pure as family stories may indicate,[2] but also the qualifications for inclusion and exclusion with defined groups shift with the times, and defined groups, of course, include a great deal of variety within those described by the label.

So too in the ancient world the lines between Jews and gentiles, *ethnos*, were more porous in some places than others.[3] That being acknowledged, Paul and many others in the first century could point to differentiations between those who considered themselves Jews and those who did not—in other words, those who believed they were biological descendants of Abraham and those who did not. Surprising to no one more than Paul, the gospel of Jesus Christ—the Jewish Messiah—cut straight through that dividing line between those two groups.

Nowhere is this more clear than in his letter to the church at Ephesus. I recognize the textual questions of this attribution, as well as the arguments against Pauline authorship, but I am convinced by my own reading as well as the arguments of many others that if any of the so-called deutero-Paulines are to be moved into his corpus, Ephesians presents the best case.[4] Even if it is not by him, however, it is Christian Scripture and therefore demands the attention of those who claim this book as their authority. As such, it also demands our obedience.

In the middle of the second chapter, Paul, for the first time, names the group to which his readers belong: "So then, remember that at one time you Gentiles by birth, called 'the uncircumcision' by those who are called 'the

1. Ok, *Constructing Ethnic Identity*, 6.

2. Ok notes, "The 'real or perceived' aspect of common blood described above is significant. It has become the consensus view among social scientists that ethnicity is socially constructed. The idea of shared descent, central to many ancient and modern conceptions of ethnic identity, is difficult, if not impossible, to ascertain. Nonetheless, its significance cannot be underestimated . . . ethnicity is an illusory concept, for all people actually do have ancestors. What is elusive about claims to shared ancestors, however, is when people choose to remember them, which ancestors they deem important, how much their idea of ancestry corresponds with the facts of ancestry, and what are the circumstances in which ethnic identity takes on greater or lesser importance" (*Constructing Ethnic Identity*, 5).

3. Gruen, *Diaspora*, 5.

4. Wright, *Paul in Fresh Perspective*, 18–19.

circumcision'—a physical circumcision made in the flesh by human hands"
(Eph 2:11).[5] Their practice with regard to what they did with their baby boys
or, better said, did *not* do marked them as "other" from the Jews. As those who
did not practice the covenant expression of circumcision, they were separated
from the Messiah, aliens from the polity of Israel, foreigners from the covenant of promise, having no hope and without God in the world (Eph 2:12).
Paul does not present himself as a suave, politically correct practitioner of
religious pluralism with a sentiment such as "Israel has our God, the gentiles
have theirs; either is fine." No, instead, he makes it very clear that the very
good things, namely, promise and hope, reside with *this* God as made known
in *this* Messiah through *this* people with *these* practices. Race and ethnicity
and religion seem one and the same. Crossing the line of one meant crossing
the line of the others.

Ephesians indicates that Paul still believes this, but he now sees the
method of change radically differently. In Christ Jesus, the gentiles, who were
far off, have been brought near by nothing less than the blood of this Messiah
(Eph 2:13). They are now in a new religion, but this has also made a difference in the conception of their ancestry as well. Paula Fredriksen describes
the thought process of the ancient world: "To change gods fully, to make an
exclusive commitment to the Jewish god and to Jewish ancestral practices was
tantamount to changing ethnicity: a pagan's 'becoming' a Jew in effect altered
his ties to his own pantheon, family, and *patria*."[6] Now these gentiles have
been brought into a new bloodline.

In the family of this Messiah, he is the peace, *our* peace, Paul says, peace
between Jew and gentile. He, the Jewish Messiah, by his crucified and resurrected Jewish flesh, takes them both, Jew and gentile, and makes them one by
destroying the dividing wall, the enmity, the barrier-created hatred that ran
between them (Eph 2:14). All of Paul's collective pronouns are gathered into
the singular: Christ. The laws that divide them include circumcision, which
marks the member of the body thought to cause the continuation of family
lines. The Messiah brings those laws to an end so that he might create from
the two one new humanity in himself, a new family at peace (Eph 2:15). He
reconciles both to God in one body through the cross, killing the enmity as he
is killed on it (Eph 2:16). He bridges the divide and breaks down the wall with
his own death, proclaiming peace to those far as well as to those near, so that
through him, both have introduction through one Spirit to the Father.

In so doing, the Messiah has changed their relationship with God
and God's people Israel. The gentiles in Christ are no longer foreigners or

---

5. All citations in this chapter are taken from the NRSV unless otherwise noted.

6. Fredriksen, "Why Should a 'Law-Free' Mission?," 642.

sojourners but are of the same polity of the saints and dwellers in the house-hold of God. They—resting upon the (Jewish) apostles and prophets and the chief cornerstone, Jesus Christ himself—are joined together with the Jews as they grow to be the holy temple in their Lord. They are all built together to be the dwelling place of God by the Spirit (Eph 2:22).

It is important to hear clearly the themes that appear again and again: two groups are now one family; enmity and division are destroyed. It is the flesh of Christ crucified and resurrected through the power of the Spirit that brings peace. That which was once denied to the gentiles by virtue of their birth is now granted to them by virtue of their new birth: participation, belonging, eternal inheritance, promise, hope, and relationship with God.

Paul gave his freedom for this good news (Eph 3:1) because God revealed it to him, the mystery that generations wished to know. The gentiles are fellow heirs and fellow members of the same body and fellow sharers of the promise in the Messiah Jesus through the gospel.

Throughout this letter, Paul speaks of the mystery on multiple occasions. It encompasses election (Eph 1:9), manifest as grace by faith and not of works (2:8–9), and the sacrificial love of Christ the bridegroom for his bride (Eph 5:32), which cultivates the practices of personal morality (Eph 4:13–15, 25–32; 5:3–5) and spiritual warfare (Eph 6:11–17). But as the highest concentration of mystery language makes clear (three of the six occurrences appear in ch. 3), any description of Paul's gospel that does not include the reconciliation of disparate racial and ethnic groups, of nothing less than justice for racialized minorities, would be a "gospel" he would not recognize, a gospel he would call false. This is the aspect of his gospel that raised eyebrows, ruffled feathers, and cost his freedom, and even so, he would not give it up. Racial reconciliation was not some afterthought to his gospel; it was the anthropological goal of his gospel—and not just in the future kingdom. The breaking down of the dividing wall was not a spiritual principle that had absolutely no impact on daily life, a bifurcation between spiritual and practical that would be totally foreign to Paul's understanding. Paul would never have tolerated the lie that hierarchical separation in real life could ever be a reflection of spiritual equality. He meant for the full-blooded gospel of racial reconciliation to be lived out *right now*. This is most readily apparent in Galatians 2, when he recounts the following event:

> But when Cephas came to Antioch, I opposed him to his face, because he stood condemned. For until certain people came from James, he used to eat with the Gentiles. But after they came, he was drawing back and kept himself separate for fear of the circumcision faction. But when I saw that they were not acting consistently

with the truth of the gospel [the truth of the mystery he laid out in Ephesians, likely], I said to Cephas before them all . . . (Gal 2:11–14)

Peter was sharing table and eating a common meal with gentiles, then stopped when it became disrespected by those who came from another place. Because of this, Paul spoke to Cephas before all and said (I paraphrase), "Are you out of your mind?" The fact that Peter would not share a meal with gentiles, would not perform the simple act of eating together—which demonstrated that Peter thought he was more clean than his fellow Christians—raised Paul's ire and demanded public rebuke from one apostle to another. Joel Willitts comments about this event, "Peter's behavior was the result *not* of wrong gospel theology, but the wrong appropriation of their shared theology to daily life."[7]

This is, of course, the same letter in which Paul proclaims that there is no longer Jew or Greek, there is no longer slave or free, there is no longer male and female because of the oneness in Christ Jesus (Gal 3:28). This encounter with Peter proves that the claim of 3:28 is christological truth with real-life implications (implications we see artfully laid out in his letter to Philemon as well).

His gospel of unity in Christ is not "pie in the sky when you die, that we'll all be together by and by."[8] Instead, he proclaims boldly that *right now* those of us in Christ will treat each other with respect in the mundane things of life. Paul can instruct Peter: you will sit at the same table with your gentile siblings.[9] How in God's name people in the past could read this letter and tolerate or even advocate for segregation in society and in their churches is, to me, incomprehensible.[10] Their blind spots are stunning.

I must acknowledge, however, that some places in the Scriptures tell slaves to obey masters (Eph 6:5; Col 3:22; Titus 2:9). In light of those, it may not be completely clear why Paul's admonitions for Jews and gentiles should apply to different gentile races in the modern world. This is a vital question.

Certainly, Paul was calling for respect and unity but did so with a clear privilege for the Jews. The gospel came to the Jews first (Rom 1:16–17); all gentiles were joining in the Jewish story (although Jews were certainly called to make compromises of their culture as well, namely, the lack of enforcement

---

7. Willitts, "Paul the Rabbi," 229.

8. Hill, "Preacher and the Slave."

9. Willitts further comments, "The truth of the gospel, on which they agree, created a new social reality. The gospel reconciles diverse ethnic communities and relativizes without erasing distinctions" ("Paul the Rabbi," 229).

10. For the biblical argument utilized for segregation, see Hawkins, *Bible Told Them So*.

for circumcision and kosher practices for gentiles now considered part of God's covenant people). Possibly it is not only the similarities to which we should pay attention—Scripture calls for real unity and real respect—but also the differences. There is a people group highlighted and prioritized in the biblical text, and that is the descendants of Abraham. Clearly, those who have been racialized as white are not equated with this group. My racial group—along with those of African, Asian, or Indigenous descent—are all, in Paul's terms, gentiles. Not only is there no room for segregation and oppression in Paul's vision of the Christian community made up of Jews and gentiles, but disrespect among gentiles, all members of the nonprivileged group, is even more ridiculous. Paul's call for lived respect between Jews and gentiles applies *even more* to groups of gentiles. Willie Jennings observes, "This first aspect of racial faith emerged from forgetting that we were Gentiles."[11] This is not to say that all of us gentiles became a homogenous group who practiced "color-blindness." Even within the gentiles, there was recognition of difference. Galatians had different issues than Corinthians, and so do we today. We can practice mutual respect by acknowledging, celebrating, and at times mourning our distinct experiences.

Lest I point the finger too vigorously to those in other times, what 2020 taught me is that I, too, had not seen Scripture in all its clarity. I had been reading this text, teaching it even, and I, too, had missed God's call concerning the gospel. The Scripture that God used to bring that home most clearly was one of the most basic in all the Bible: love your neighbor as yourself (Mark 12:31). I was led to this text by another, the section of John 13–15 where Jesus says repeatedly, "I give you a new commandment, that you love one another. Just as I have loved you, you also should love one another" (John 13:34) and "This is my commandment, that you love one another as I have loved you" (John 15:12).

It was my turn in the preaching rotation the first Sunday in June, and we were in this portion of John. I had been inspired by my colleague Esau McCaulley's sermon on the fires of Pentecost the week before[12] and awakened by conversations with students and friends as we processed the events around us. It seemed to me that on this day I could not be silent about the hideous murder of George Floyd. What I realized is that I live differently than some of my neighbors. I'm not nervous to go running in my neighborhood. I don't get pulled over regularly, even though it is quite accurate that I am speeding most of the time. Before June of 2020, I had some knowledge of these things but never had really stared them in the face. And this is key: I had not done

11. Jennings, "Overcoming Racial Faith," 6.
12. McCaulley, "Flames of Pentecost."

anything about them. God convicted me that my lack of love for my neighbor was demonstrated not through sins of commission—again, I wasn't a segregationist—but rather through sins of omission. I was vincibly ignorant, which means that I did not recognize something as an injustice, but I should have. I had a responsibility to know—and probably opportunities to know—that *x* is unjust but had failed to pay attention to that knowledge.[13]

Before the summer of 2020, I had not really paid attention, and therefore I had not used whatever influence I possessed to join in the work for changes so that, ultimately, the experience of our community would be less racialized for minorities. The push of the Scriptures I had studied for decades met the pull of the cultural awakening around me.

I still have many questions and feel unsure if I am proceeding in the right way or doing enough. I worry that I might fall back again into vincible ignorance. In the midst of preparing this paper, I preached in Wheaton's chapel on Ephesians 1, and I realized what Paul prayed for the Ephesians was that they would have more of God. I've made that my prayer for myself as well, and if I am growing in wisdom and revelation in the knowledge of our Savior, I can rest assured that I will grow in the lived knowledge of loving my neighbor. If I am listening to God, the God who broke down the wall will not allow me, through action or inaction, to build it up again.

MADISON N. PIERCE

In early spring of 2019, I received an email from my friend and coauthor Amy Peeler. She shared that she, Esau McCaulley, Janette Ok, and Osvaldo Padilla were putting together a single-volume multiethnic commentary on the New Testament and wanted me to contribute. My instinct was to say *absolutely!* After all, to collaborate with these editors alone was a dream come true. But then I felt conflicted . . . Would a nonwhite scholar be better? Have we not heard enough from *us*—white scholars? But within the invitation, it was reiterated that "White" is a racialized category, and I recognized the value there might be in *naming* how my Whiteness affected my experience and reading of the text. In my commentary, I would try to set aside the privilege of being "default" and acknowledge my situatedness more readily. This chapter is a reflection on my experience of writing a socially-located commentary on the Epistle to the Hebrews.

I worked on the final chapter of Hebrews on the day that George Floyd was murdered. I then spent the next week watching the news while editing

---

13. Thank you to my colleague Ty Kieser for this insight.

my submission. I had committed to a June 1 deadline, but now I hated every word on the pages. I prayed. I wept. I wrote some *very* angry words. That week transformed my commentary.

One passage that served as the focus of those prayers, tears, and emotions was Hebrews 2. I'll describe some of those developments shortly, but first, let me offer a quick summary of the chapter and an even quicker summary of some of the relevant interpretive questions.

The humanity of Jesus is likely fully in view throughout the opening chapter of Hebrews; however, the author turns his attention to humans more explicitly at the end of a series of scriptural references and, in doing so, makes several points regarding their relationship to angels. After his quotation of Ps 110:1 in Heb 1:13, the author asks, "Are not all angels ministering spirits sent to serve those who will inherit salvation?" (Heb 1:14 NIV). This question reminds the addressees that, despite their strength and longevity, angels serve humans, not the other way around.

The connection between this verse about the angels and the section that follows is often obscured by our modern chapter divisions, so let me read the texts in sequence: "Are not all angels ministering spirits sent to serve those who will inherit salvation? *For this reason*, we must pay careful attention to what we have heard" (Heb 1:14).[14] In other words, since the angels serve us, we need to live faithfully. We need to take seriously our inheritance. After this exhortation and its development, the author returns to his comparison between humans and angels. He says, "[God] has not subjected the world to come to angels" (Heb 2:5).

This reinforces the author's prior point about the importance of humanity within God's overall design. Thus, contrary to many who see the author's use of Psalm 8 as serving his Christology first and foremost, I think the author underscores God's promise to humanity with the psalm—a reading more consistent within its original context within the Hebrew Bible. To be clear, I do think the author is making a *broadly* christological point through the psalm, but he does that by building upon an established anthropological use of the psalm. More precisely, the psalm remains predominantly anthropological, even if it is used for ultimately christological purposes.[15]

The quotation says, "What is man [or human beings] that you are mindful" (Heb 2:6). And indeed, within extrabiblical literature, at various points in Jewish interpretive history, angels said this very thing to God as they saw him

14. Scripture quotations are my own translation, unless otherwise noted.

15. For a fuller discussion of my reading of this text, see Pierce, *Divine Discourse*, 92–98.

prioritize human beings: when he created Adam,[16] when he made the promise to Abraham,[17] when he gave the law to Moses.[18] In these instances, the angels were envious. After all, it is not to them that God has subjected the world to come; instead, he has subjected it to us.

But perhaps God subjecting the world to come to human beings seems unlikely to you. To understand fully how plausible this claim is—or isn't—we must consider how it coheres with the rest of the letter.

In Hebrews, the inheritance of God's children is expansive. In 1:14, they inherit "salvation," and elsewhere they are said to inherit "promises" (6:12; cf. 6:17; 11:9), "righteousness" (11:7), and finally, a "kingdom that cannot be shaken" (12:28). These ideas fit together, of course, representing a full picture of what they will receive alongside how they will be restored. But the last of these things—"a kingdom that cannot be shaken" (12:28)—surely is in large part coterminous with the "world to come." It is a world in which the Son reigns supreme—alongside his human brothers and sisters.

In some ways, this promise that we will inherit the coming kingdom is within Psalm 8:

> [6] What is humankind that you are mindful of them,
>   a son of man that you care for him?
> [7] You made them a little lower than the angels;
>   you crowned them with glory and honor
> [8] and put everything under their feet. (quoted in Heb 2:6–8)

Although this is a picture of the dominion afforded to all humanity at creation, some people expand the idea of ruling in ways that God does not intend. The creation mandate is not a challenge to gain dominion, as though the world were one big game of Risk; no, this is a portrait of *shared* responsibility for all of humanity as we steward the resources that God has given us. But clearly a misunderstanding of God's intention prevails. At best, it appears that some think that the creation mandate—to rule over creatures—applies to them *more*, which of course means that it applies to some others *less*. At worst, some think that the creation mandate gives them license not only to rule "over the fish in the sea and the birds in the air" but over fellow image-bearers too. And, of course, in our nation's history, there was previously a literal enslavement of image-bearers. However, what we need to come to terms with are the subtle ways that we exercise control over fellow image-bearers *today*. And, to borrow from the author of Hebrews, "as long as it is called 'today,' encourage one

---

16. *b. Sanh.* 38b; *Gen. Rab.* 8:5–6.

17. See Spiegel, *Last Trial*; Bernstein, "Angels at the Aqedah."

18. See Moffitt, *Atonement*, 154n12.

another so that none of you may be hardened by sin's deceitfulness" (3:13)— deceitfulness that too often excuses our complicity.

These dynamics are, of course, products of the fall. But Hebrews 2 begins a bit earlier in the biblical narrative, offering a picture of humanity that begins, well, at the beginning. This is not to say that Hebrews imagines a return to the garden, full stop. There is restoration as well as consummation in view.

This is all good news. But somehow, as I began to edit my commentary in the week following the murder of George Floyd, Hebrews 2 made me sick. Suddenly, *submission* and being granted the power to rule didn't feel like good news, particularly because of its abusive possibilities. Coming from my own background, as a ministry-oriented woman in the Southern Baptist Convention, I had worked *so* hard to see value in submission—a very biblical concept that had been weaponized against me. I had worked to see beyond silence and complicity and to see instead service in love, washing feet, laying down lives, having the same mind as Christ Jesus. I also had worked *so* hard to understand the goodness of honor and the related term *power*, despite the abuses that I had personally experienced.

But now, despite my work to understand these concepts in a faithful way, I saw evil in those words again. I saw the subjection of my Black brothers and sisters. I saw my own power that I had failed to acknowledge and the ways that I had placed those co-heirs under *my* feet.

Before that day, in my draft of the commentary, I had written something about the value of recognizing that Jesus is a representative of *all* humanity— male and female, Jewish and not.

Those things are true, of course. But what struck me in a new way as I edited my draft was Jesus *sharing. Everything.*

Ruling as co-heirs in Christ means nothing that is inherited is diminished by sharing. In my experience, so often White Christians are afraid of sharing. We think of too much as a zero-sum game. If we invite someone from a traditionally underrepresented background to lead, then we might be displaced. If we offer them resources, then we might lose some of ours. If we center their perspectives, then we might become marginalized.

Even *if* those things were true, God forbid we endure what our sisters and brothers who have been enslaved and oppressed on the basis of race have always lived out.

When I returned to Hebrews 2 last May, I saw a radically different picture in the person of Christ. The Son of God, the firstborn who was guaranteed an inheritance, shared in our blood and flesh so that he might serve—*die*—on our behalf.

Did he do this for his own glory?

Did he do this to increase his own status?

Of course not. He did this *for us*—in part so that we might become inheritors alongside him. But we've heard these words before again and again. So let me reframe that slightly: Jesus died so that he could share *his* inheritance and glory with us. For the joy set before him (Heb 12:2), he suffered, offering himself up, so that we could have what was previously just his. Of course, the inheritance and vast riches of God's blessings are truly beyond measure. Like a meal of loaves and fish, everyone can have their fill, and yet still there is abundance.

But there is more. Alongside the promises of Hebrews 2, to which we will return shortly, there is an acknowledgement of the current reality. Heb 2:8 says, "We do not yet see all things in subjection." Of course this is true. Look around.

Nevertheless, my theology urges me toward an understanding of the world that takes seriously the work of Jesus to restore the world in the here and the now. The kingdom of God is indeed near. But alongside that, I recognize that the world was so deeply marred by the fall that it has a very long way to go before it reflects the goodness that God intends for it.

We see this tension in the promises about status in the New Testament. As Dr. Peeler has highlighted, Paul says in Eph 2:14–15 that Jesus "destroyed the dividing wall of hostility . . . creating one new humanity."

And he says in Gal 3:28 (NIV) that "there is neither Jew nor Gentile, neither slave nor free, nor is there male and female, for you are all one in Christ Jesus."

But we do not yet see all things in submission. We do not yet see *all* dividing walls destroyed. And we do not yet see all people being treated as though they are equal heirs of God's promises.

I would encourage us, especially us White Christians, as we go out into the world, to remember that these promises *are* indeed fully realized, but they are by no means fully *experienced*.

We do not yet see all things in submission to the will of God. Instead, we subjugate, we diminish, and we try to veil the glory and honor of our sisters and brothers.

But we do see Jesus.

We fix our eyes on the one who has gone before us. One who, according to the author of Hebrews, is not ashamed—is, in fact, *proud*—to call us brothers and sisters.

He shared in our humanity and was tested in every way. For those among us who have endured unthinkable racial trauma or who have had to normalize and disregard constant microaggressions or who have wept with their children when they experienced this wickedness, Jesus shared that too. Paraphrasing Hebrews 12, he shared in our pain for the sake of the joy set before him—the possibility that he might join together in celebration with angels and archangels and the assembly of the firstborn.

Since Jesus shared in our humanity in order to make us co-heirs, we are also called to share in the sufferings of our fellow humans to make evident that we are *co*-heirs. Jesus invites us to share in the sufferings of one another, to the extent that we are able, so that we, too, might be merciful and faithful to one another—just like our Great High Priest.

These texts of the New Testament proclaim that we must suffer together—to intervene when we are able, to advocate for more just policies in our spheres, to listen, and to allow our hearts to be changed. We must remember that the dividing wall hurts *everyone*—not just those outside it.

BIBLIOGRAPHY

Bernstein, Moshe. "Angels at the Aqedah: A Study in the Development of a Midrashic Motif." *Dead Sea Discoveries* 7 (2000) 263–91.

Fredriksen, Paula. "Why Should a 'Law-Free' Mission Mean a 'Law-Free' Apostle?" *JBL* 134 (2015) 637–50.

Gruen, Erich S. *Diaspora: Jews amidst Greeks and Romans.* Cambridge, MA: Harvard University Press, 2002.

Hawkins, J. Russell. *The Bible Told Them So: How Southern Evangelicals Fought to Preserve White Supremacy.* Oxford: Oxford University Press, 2021.

Hill, Joe. "The Preacher and the Slave." *Protest Song Lyrics*, 1911. http://www.protestsonglyrics.net/Miscellaneous_Songs/Preacher-Slave.phtml.

Jennings, Willie. "Overcoming Racial Faith." *Divinity* 14 (2015) 4–9.

McCaulley, Esau. "The Flames of Pentecost, a World on Fire, and the Hope of the Kingdom." *Esau McCaulley* (blog), 31 May 2020. http://esaumccaulley.com/the-flames-of-pentecost-a-world-on-fire-and-the-hope-of-the-kingdom/.

Moffitt, David M. *Atonement and the Logic of Resurrection in the Epistle to the Hebrews.* NovTSup 141. Leiden: Brill, 2011.

Neusner, Jacob, trans. *Mishnah: A New Translation.* New Haven: Yale University Press, 1988.

Ok, Janette. *Constructing Ethnic Identity in 1 Peter: Who You Are No Longer.* LNTS 645. London: T. & T. Clark, 2021.

Pierce, Madison N. *Divine Discourse in the Epistle to the Hebrews: The Recontextualization of Spoken Quotations of Scripture.* SNTSMS 178. Cambridge: Cambridge University Press, 2020.

Spiegel, Shalom. *The Last Trial: On the Legends and Lore of the Command to Abraham to Offer Isaac as a Sacrifice: The Akedah.* New York: Behrman, 1979.

Willitts, Joel. "Paul the Rabbi of Messianic Judaism: Reading the Antioch Incident within Judaism as an Irreducibility Story." *JSPL* 6 (2016) 225–47.

Wright, N. T. *Paul in Fresh Perspective.* Minneapolis: Fortress, 2009.

4

Embracing the Other to the Glory of God

A Pre-Justice Idea (with Some Help from Invisible Man)

ERIC C. REDMOND

INTRODUCTION

ROMANS 16 LOOKS LIKE a simple list of hellos and benedictions appropriate for the end of a first-century letter. *Greet this person, say hello to that one, tell these friends hi from me, remember that one named Narcissus* (who has a very unfortunate name). Most of it is so pedestrian that we do not give it the attention we give to the Romans Road evangelistic passages, the Golden Chain of salvation in Romans 8, the meaning of *dikaiosynê theou* or *dikaiothentes ek pisteos*, related New Perspective debates, and the practical discussions on a living-sacrifice lifestyle in Rom 12–15.

Yet significant to Paul's argument about the revelation of the gospel of God and the obedience of faith is his call for the *affectionate greeting of people* according to both spiritual and social identities. The end of this letter is not an appendage to the gospel discussion but a challenge to live out the gospel to its full conclusions. One might even consider chapter 16 to be the capstone of the working out of the gospel as manifested in Romans, for what Paul calls the believers to do in these greetings grows only from the rich soil of the mercies of God.

When we have the practice of affectionately—even physically (Rom 16:16!)—embracing fellow believers, including those new to us, we are doing so as a necessary outworking of the mystery of the gospel, for the sake of God's glory among all peoples. That is, *we are embracing the other to the glory of God.*

In demonstrating this aspect of the practical application of the gospel, Paul will reveal five things about embracing fellow believers, with particular reference to social identities. As we are working through the passage, I will utilize Paul's argument to bring in an important idea related to social identity, visibility, and justice from Ralph Ellison's *Invisible Man.* It is my belief that Paul's directives here provide us with pre-justice seeds—seeds of a Christian ethos and pathos that march in front of justice.[1]

EMBRACING MEANS: VALUING THE CONTRIBUTIONS WOMEN MAKE TO THE WORK OF THE GOSPEL

Rom 16:1–2

Paul commends Phoebe to the church, and she probably is the bearer of the letter, as some scholars propose.[2] She is unknown to the believers at Rome, and Paul is supplying credentials for her to be accepted, so that the church does not need to wonder if they are being deceived by someone with ill motives and only claiming to be a believer. Paul gives his good name to her rather than letting her work to earn the respect of believers in Rome.[3]

Imagine if Phoebe had arrived before the congregation in Rome as a believer, but without Paul's commendation. She would have been just another woman believer and possibly would have received cordial treatment. But she was also single, for she was traveling alone, and no husband was mentioned

---

1. I will expand the exposition of the first three sections and minimize the exposition of the last two sections for the sake of space limitations.

2. Moo, *Epistle to the Romans,* 913; Schreiner, *Romans,* 759.

3. I discuss a matter of gender justice first because it presents itself first in the passage. However, rightly and wisely, efforts on racial and gender justice should work together to undo the misuse of power that makes possible inequities toward both women and people of color. For more reasoning on the need for racial and gender effort to strive together, see Ellens and Davis, "Intersection of Gender"; Entralgo, "Eviction Crisis"; Frye, "Racism and Sexism Combine"; Asare, "Gender Equity Is Useless"; Li, "Recent Developments"; Patel, "Notes on Gender."

as with the wives greeted below.[4] So her reception may have come coolly. But with Paul's words, she comes with high marks that she should be revered by all.

Paul first introduces her as "our sister" (1a), denoting her as a member adopted by Christ into the family of God like Paul and the other Roman believers. The work of Christ in her should be a priority in the way the assembly is to receive the previously unknown Phoebe; *she is a new face to them but is their Christ-purchased sister by divine adoption*. Schreiner notes that the term "'sister' relays the intimacy and warmth characterizing the early church so that the relationship between family members describes most appropriately the affiliation between Christians."[5] Therefore, what Paul says below will not contradict the intimacy and warmth expected between believers.

Second, the apostle describes her as a "servant at Cenchreae" (1b), indicating that she ministers in the vein of our Lord. Both Schreiner and Moo argue that Phoebe held the office of deacon, even though both scholars caution us on thinking of fully developed offices at this point in the church's early history and formation.[6] "Servant (*diakonon*) of the church at Cenchreae" suggests a special capacity, especially as this is Paul's first use of "church" in the letter.[7]

Third, he informs the church to receive her with worth—worth that they show to one another as saints (2a). They are to refrain from treating her as an outsider or view her with suspicion. Instead, they must regard her as one "in the Lord," as a fellow Christian in whom the gospel is working.

Fourth, the apostle instructs the church to provide for her needs—whatever need she might have—in reciprocation for the ministry support she has given to Paul and others as a patron or benefactor (*prostatis*) so that the gospel might go forth (2b–c). In whatever matter she might have need, they are to help this sister, deacon, and woman of high social standing and wealth.[8] Here Paul refers to financial items and not simply faith items. Phoebe uses her patronage (social) for the kingdom (spiritual). In all, Paul provides authority for Phoebe to be received with dignity. He will recognize the many things that demand respect socially and spiritually rather than allowing the Roman believers to reduce her to a culturally misinformed, gender-based status only.

---

4. Paul mentions "Prisca and Aquila" (3) and "Andronicus and Junia" (7).

5. Schreiner, *Romans*, 759.

6. Moo, *Epistle to the Romans*, 914; Schreiner, *Romans*, 760–61.

7. Schreiner writes, "The designation 'deacon of the church in Cenchreae' suggests that Phoebe served in this special capacity, since this is the only occasion in which the term διάκονος is linked with a particular local church" (*Romans*, 760).

8. On Phoebe as one with wealth, see Moo, *Epistle to the Romans*, 916.

My church—Calvary Memorial Church, Oak Park, Illinois—is comple-mentarian in our view of the role of men and women in the church and home. Unfortunately, this theological position contributes to many blind spots with respect to some of our insensitivities toward women.[9] The position often leaves women in congregations like ours asking how they can serve in the congrega-tion with *all* their magnificent gifts, education, experiences, skills, and talents.

Rather than making a list of roles that are appropriate, following Paul's call to the saints at Rome, we all need to continue to work on actions that value women's full packages of gifts, including providing leadership in some roles that traditionally have been limited to men—limited for reasons that have nothing to do with the order of creation. In all our congregations, our hope should be that all women entering our assemblies will sense that we are welcoming and valuing them as people of dignity.

We should hope that single women like Phoebe will feel we are esteem-ing them as much as married women, and vice versa, as Paul does in this passage. We should strive to see that a married women's worth is not reduced to the ability to bear children and raise exceptional students, and that a single women's worth is not minimized to a wrongly assumed freedom to provide childcare at will and an availability to wed our sons who are still single in their thirties, forties, and fifties.

EMBRACING MEANS: RECOGNIZING SOCIAL IDENTITIES TO DEMONSTRATE THE AFFECTION OF THE GOSPEL

Rom 16:3–16

This list of greetings is full of hellos to gospel workers, people in house church-es, fellow Jewish believers, those who worked hard, and many family relation-ships. "Greetings express the love that was the mark of the early Christian community."[10]

Several writers have noted the number of women in this list, which argues against Paul having chauvinistic tendencies. Most significantly, the greetings are tender, full of Paul's emotions and affections toward believers in Rome. Of the eighteen Greek names, eight Latin names, seven Jewish names, three names from slave households, and six names of persons who probably

---

9. Most notably, see the corrections offered in Barr, *Making of Biblical Womanhood*; Byrd, *Recovering from Biblical Manhood*; Du Mez, *Jesus and John Wayne*.

10. Schreiner, *Romans*, 763.

were slaves,[11] I will focus on three sets of believers in the list while briefly mentioning the others and making a notation on the slavery-related persons.

First, Prisca (a.k.a. Priscilla) and Aquila are a wife-and-husband team well known in the New Testament as companions of Paul.[12] Paul identifies them to the Roman congregation as people who risked their lives on his behalf, and people for whom churches in Galatia, Philippi, Thessalonica, Berea, and Athens gave thanks (vv. 3–4). The greeting invites the Romans to ask Prisca and Aquila *how* they saved Paul's life and *why* the churches give thanks for them—things that would be dear to Prisca and Aquila's hearts. They also have opportunity to feel the heart of Paul, for one cannot speak of people risking their lives while being stoic in one's emotions. It is not "They risked their lives for me." Instead, it is "They risked their lives for me!"

Second, skipping to verse 7, Paul introduces the reader to the husband-and-wife team of Andronicus and Junia (7). They come with four descriptors: 1) they are his Jewish kinsmen (7b), which Paul could have left out so as not to draw attention to their Judaism, but he included it for recognition; 2) they have spent time in prison (7b), so the Romans learn that they have suffered for the sake of the gospel; 3) they have a high reputation among all of the apostles (7b), that is, the apostles think much of them, so the Romans should too; and 4) they were converted to Christ prior to Paul (7c), *which means their maturity and length of time in Christ should be honored in the eyes of their brothers and sisters.* Note, I am not entering the debate about the type of apostleship held by Andronicus and Junia.[13] The fact that Paul recognizes them affectionately is what is important in this discussion.

If one were to think that here we have an example of Paul "respecting persons," then this whole chapter needs to be scrapped, for the majority of the list is a brag fest. Instead, *Paul is showing us that the gospel can embrace people without turning us into people-pleasers or people who are favorably biased to some and not others.*

Third, in verse 13, there are Rufus and his mother. Describing Rufus as "chosen in the Lord" harkens back to Rom 11:5 and believing Israel's identity as a remnant "chosen by grace." But the identity of Rufus's mother as one who mothered Paul speaks to her caring nature and not of her elect status; it is not "mother in Christ" but "mother to me." The church should look at Rufus's mother as one whose walk with Christ expressed itself in nurturing care for

11. Schreiner, *Romans*, 763.

12. See Acts 18:2, 18, 26; 1 Cor 16:19; 2 Tim 4:19.

13. For more on both the debate and the gender identity of Junia, see Burer and Wallace, "Was Junia Really an Apostle?"; Burk, "Junia Is a Woman"; Moo, *Epistle to the Romans*, 921–24; Schreiner, *Romans*, 768–71.

the apostle and possibly for others who would travel to Rome in need of such care. Paul approves of mothering another as honorable gospel work, being one who had benefited from such love.

With respect to slavery, Ampliatus (8a), Persis (12c), Tryphaena (12b), Tryphosa (12b), Hermes (14c), and Nereus (15c) all carried names common for slaves and freedmen in the empire.[14] Herodion (11a) would have been a Jewish freedman who formerly served the household of Herod. Paul includes them among those he greets without calling attention to their present or former slave statuses. In contrast, he highlights their "fidelity to Christ" (10) and their dear friendship in the Lord (8). Seemingly, Paul avoids a diminutive association when greeting them, so that they will not be looked upon with asterisks next to their names rather than as those greeted like Prisca and Aquila (3a), Mary (6a), and Apelles (10a).

Schreiner notes two important things of this list in 16:3–16. First, "by commending them, Paul allies himself with them and encourages the Romans to value them."[15] What should the Romans value? In his role as ally, Paul encourages the Roman believers to value things like, "risked their lives for me," and "mother to me," both of which are *social* identifiers.

Second, without the emphasis I am giving presently, Schreiner says, "Greetings are not merely secular 'hellos' but are rooted in the new life of Christ. Moreover, the Christian gospel was not a cause or ideology that trampled the personhood of individuals."[16] Schreiner is right: personhood, including all our positive social identifiers, is to be welcomed rather than crushed, flattened, run over, squashed, stepped on, or violated.

Verse 16 allows all believers to test our ability to embrace fellow saints fully: "Greet one another with a holy kiss. All the churches of Christ greet you."

The holy kiss was more than a casual greeting like a fist bump, bro-hug, or Baptist pseudo-kiss greeting with one's cheek partially turned away from the would-be greeter. One also should not think of some French, Spanish, or Middle Eastern traditions in which greetings with kisses do not denote feelings of great affection. Rather, one should think of hugging or kissing the parent, child, grandchild, or best friend (other than one's spouse) you love and have not seen for weeks or months. When you finally see that loved one in person, you give a greeting that is not sexual but is full of affection. The holy kiss was "an expression of the oneness of people who represent different social classes, and it expresses the warmth and love transcending gender, religious,

---

14. Moo, *Epistle to the Romans*, 924–26.

15. Schreiner, *Romans*, 764. Schreiner references Stenschke, "'Your Obedience Is Known.'"

16. Schreiner, *Romans*, 764.

national, or ethnic divisions."[17] "Holy" would make sure that the natural kiss on the lips or cheeks did not hint at sexual expression.

Could you give *every* believer the affectionate hug you would give to that beloved friend or relative absent from your life for months, simply because the person is a believer? For almost all of us, the answer would be no. For it is not our identities as "saints" that stops us from greeting one another.

If we looked at everyone only through the lenses of spiritual identity, we would holy-kiss every member of Christ—or, at least, every member within an assembly, as Paul instructs the Romans—for all would be blood-bought, united mysteriously to Christ, filled with the Holy Spirit, holding the promise of gaining and being the inheritance of God. But we do not kiss all adult members of a congregation in this way. Why? Because among our fellow members, *his beard itches, she has bad breath, he gives you the creeps, her eyes look funny, he doesn't wash his hands when he goes to the bathroom even during a pandemic, she always has dandruff on her clothes, and you once saw a bug crawling in her hair when you were sitting in the row behind her!*

We look at the human aspects of the saints of God in the pews next to us when challenged to offer simple greetings. Therefore, what makes us think we are any less cautious in recognizing other aspects of human identities—social aspects? *He has a degree from Aberdeen or the University of Chicago Medicine, she commutes into the city to work from a rich town in exurbia, he was a Navy Seal, she used to be a member of a cult, he never finished school, his parents were abusive, she was loose when she was a teenager,* and so on. We should not begin to say to ourselves that we do not make such evaluations every day. All believers do the same.

Paul indicates that the gospel should shape how we make such evaluations, so that we can fully embrace all the saints of God with full holiness and full affection. Then it will not seem odd for members of another congregation to send full greetings to us as if we have been close siblings all our lives—that is, "all the churches of Christ greet [you, Romans]" (16:16).

Again, Paul's call is to welcome with the holy kiss the one who mothered him when he needed mothering; they are to welcome the mothering one affectionately. Paul's call is to finish reading Romans, look at the new-to-them letter carrier, and get up and physically embrace her as one who was a patron of Paul. Paul's call is to look at the household slaves in the letter and not call attention to their present or former statuses as slaves but rather embrace them as members of the house churches, giving them the same holy kisses the household owners would receive.

17. Schreiner, *Romans*, 772.

Embracing Means: Avoiding Those Acting Like Satan, for They Are Against the Gospel

Rom 16:17–20 and the Eulogy of Tod Clifton

For Paul, there are some on whom we should not bestow a holy kiss—some we should not embrace. In every congregation, believers are to watch for people who claim to be protecting the church but are protecting private agendas and personal preferences. They create stumbling blocks to gospel fidelity and growth.[18] If someone calls for a gathering in a home or location other than the church to discuss matters of concern within the congregation before approaching the leadership with the concerns, that might be the first step toward division, and that person probably is not serving Christ.

Such persons might make the invitation to meet with them seem necessary to save the church from people steering it the wrong way or from heretical teachings. They can use enticing words so polished that they could also convince you of the necessity of buying an igloo in Miami. This means one needs wisdom to complement a mature faith and trust in the authority of the Scriptures; believers cannot be naïve about people having personal agendas or be unwilling to lose friendships. Some of our friends will err here, providing words of urgency that amount to divisiveness and rebellion, and it happens in the soundest evangelical churches under the guise of righteousness.

If those causing divisions were obvious, we could stop them readily. "Oh, look! Three-fourths of the middle-aged families with teens are rebelling against the vision for high school ministry, for they are refusing to let their children participate until they make Bible drill competitions mandatory again!" If divisions were that obvious, we would not need wisdom. We simply would not embrace that behavior.

But we tend to get it wrong in churches. We embrace divisive behavior by allowing it to remain and fester but hesitate to embrace God-fearing saints who have a social status that rests outside of our comfort zones.

Here is where I need to invite Ralph Ellison into the discussion. In 1952, Ellison published *Invisible Man*, a work that won the National Book Award. Now a classic, *Invisible Man* follows an unnamed protagonist whose life explores what it means to be invisible in society because of one's race.

---

18. Those causing dissensions are doing so to people who have "learned teaching." They are deceiving believers, not unbelievers. Paul's admonition is toward believers and their development. Secondarily, however, it is true that if they have the wrong gospel, they would not share the gospel accurately or at all.

Rather than describing African American life as having a veil of darkness over everything, like W. E. B. DuBois, Ellison describes African American life as having invisibility in society. As Ellison's protagonist says,

> I am invisible, understand, simply because people refuse to see me. . . . When they approach me, they see only my surroundings, themselves, or figments of their imagination—indeed, everything and anything except me. . . . That invisibility to which I refer occurs because of a peculiar disposition of the eyes of those with whom I come in contact. A matter of the construction of their *inner* eyes, those eyes with which they look through their physical eyes upon reality. . . . You wonder whether you aren't simply a phantom in other people's minds.[19]

So, for Ellison, invisibility occurs when people with their physical eyes fail to look upon African Americans and see a person of worth and dignity rather than seeing a threatening phantom who is simply a part of a class known as "Negro" in Ellison's 1952 language.

Late in the work in chapter 20, invisibility will contribute to the death of a young African American man at the hands of the NYPD in Harlem. The scene reads much like an early twenty-first-century national racial injustice tragedy. The young Tod Clifton is being pushed and shoved by an officer who wants him to stop selling his Sambo dolls on the street corners. Seemingly in frustration and self-defense, Clifton dodges a shove intended for him, returning a punch to the police officer that sends the officer backward, off his feet, and onto the ground. The officer then pulls out his gun and shoots the unarmed Clifton, and Clifton dies on the scene. The protagonist witnesses the physical match and the shooting, walking away with confusion, disbelief, grief, and anger. He wanted to help his dying friend, but the officer waved off his help.

In the following chapter, the invisible protagonist is called upon to eulogize the slain young adult and community leader. He begins the eulogy of his friend with a general introduction for any dead man. To Ellison's lead character, *the certainty of the death of the unnamed man without any hope of a resurrection encore challenges the hearers to leave their hopes for more and to go home to forget about this man.* Here he is in his own words to the throngs gathered for the Harlem funeral:

> What are you waiting for me to tell you. . . ? What good will it do. . . ? Or do you expect to see some magic, the dead rise up and walk again? Go home, he's as dead as he'll ever die. That's the end

---

19. Ellison, *Invisible Man*, 1; emphasis added.

in the beginning, and there's no encore. There'll be no miracles, and there's no one here to preach a sermon. Go home, forget him. He's inside this box, newly dead. Go home and don't think about him. He's dead and you've got all you can do to think about you.[20]

Like the words "forget him," the invisible protagonist will repeat "forget it" two more times in the next paragraph, as if the hearers will be able to forget the hopeless injustice served to Clifton. Yet, when the crowd does not disperse but waits for more to be said about the slain young man, the protagonist begins to enter the name of the dead with identifying social marks. In doing so, he takes the recipient of injustice and raises him from commonality and invisibility to uniqueness and visibility. Here are his words again, at length:

All right, you do the listening in the sun, and I'll try to tell you in the sun. Then you go home and forget it. Forget it. His name was Clifton, and they shot him down. His name was Clifton, and he was tall and some folks thought him handsome. . . . Have you got it? Can you see him? Think of your brother or your cousin John. . . . He thought about things, and he felt deeply. I won't call him noble because what's such a word to do with one of us? His name was Clifton, Tod Clifton, and, like any man, he was born of woman to live awhile and fall and die. So that's his tale to the minute. So why are you waiting? You've heard it all. Why wait for more when all I can do is repeat it?[21]

But the protagonist does more than repeat it. He expands upon it, showing that Tod Clifton was not obscure or just commonly born of woman. He was unique in every way. He was not invisible to Ralph Ellison's invisible narrator. He was someone to be seen, even though the police who shot him and the listening crowd thought of him in the concept of "another Negro." Ellison intends to show the crowd that what will make the difference between a black man in the crosshairs of police living and dying unjustly is knowing there is an individual with beautiful features and detailed gifts living among us. The eulogizer does not honor a dead black street worker; he resurrects a different picture to show us the brilliance of a jewel that had lived among us.

Twenty-three times the narrator will insert the name Tod Clifton and make this invisible slain man visible to every eye and ear in the funeral crowd. For Ellison, we can forget the Tod Cliftons only if we do not see them for the unique persons of worth that they are. As we see Tod Clifton, we will see individual Asian Americans who are receiving slow or no justice in response to

20. Ellison, *Invisible Man*, 353–55.

21. Ellison, *Invisible Man*, 355.

increased attacks against them because of a term of ignorance like *China flu*.[22] We will see Sandra Bland, Philando Castile, Adam Toledo, Ahmaud Arbery, and the role of these persons in society with relational and aesthetic individuality that is not to be overlooked by any.[23]

Ellison's *Invisible Man* protagonist sees a whole person and embraces him. Paul calls us to see social identities and embrace whole persons with the sort of embracing that strives both to prevent and honor the deaths of the Tod Cliftons of this nation.

This calls for courage: *embrace the right people, and beware of the Satanlike people.* Do not simply look for doctrinal errors; look for errors in the way members treat one another within an assembly. When Paul says "watch out" for people of selfish appetites who cause divisions and dissensions, this is the purse-clutching, walk-to-the-other-side-of-the-street, keep-your-children-from-them, move-from-their-neighborhood stuff. If we can get this right in the church, we will have eyes to be wise toward what is good and innocent toward what is evil—that is, to be just and righteous toward all persons, both inside and outside of the body of Christ.

Moreover, Paul affirms that Christ intends to fulfill the promise of Gen 3:15 soon and bruise the head of the serpent with finality. Paul's words are directed at the assembly: *in every congregation, the Lord will deal with those who are the cause of dissensions, both doctrinal and otherwise.* This is his church and his gospel; it is he who wants us to embrace as Paul embraces and avoid those who are against the Lord and his bride.

Embracing Means: Promoting Our Earthly Identities to Believers so We Can Advance the Gospel

Rom 16:21–23

In these three short verses, the believers in Rome would know that if ever they were in Corinth, they had some sisters and brothers in Christ who would welcome them. While Timothy is a traveling companion of Paul, the remaining

---

22. For more on injustices toward Asian Americans stoked by use of the term *China flu*, see Fadel, "With Racial Attacks"; Itkowitz, "Trump Again Uses"; Petri and Slotnik, "Attacks on Asian-Americans"; Yam, "Trump Can't Claim 'Kung Flu'"; Zhou, "Trump's Racist References."

23. For a review of African Americans wrongly killed in race-related acts of violence, see Code Switch, "Decade of Watching," and *The New Yorker*, "Kadir Nelson's 'Say Their Names.'"

names seem to represent believers in Corinth—the place from which Paul writes Romans. This list includes the writer of the letter (Tertius), a man who can provide lodging and hospitality (Gaius), and the city treasurer (Erastus).

This is the flip side of embracing believers socially because of the gospel—the side that we all hope to experience when necessary. When your adult child, like two of my adult children, accepts work in cities far from home, you pray and hope that believers in those new regions will welcome them, befriending them. If your daughter is a doctor, you might hope other Christian doctors will welcome her into fellowship; if your child is moving as a family, you might look for your Christian contacts in the new city that can bring them into fellowship in a solid church. Letting the congregation in Rome know that Corinth's city treasurer—a social identity—is a team player for the gospel is significant.

Five years ago, our oldest child moved from the East Coast to the West Coast to take her first position after finishing law school. The primary concern my wife and I had for her was to plant herself in a healthy church that would support her spiritual growth. A second concern we had was for her to find believers in her field who could show her the practice of law from a Christian worldview. So, what did we do as her parents? We prayed, and then immediately we went online to see if we could find potential churches. *We also picked up the phone and called believing friends to ascertain who had other believing friends in our daughter's new city.*

What did we expect to happen? We expected to find connections for the benefit of our daughter's growth. Believers we had never met, but who were making themselves known to us, received our daughter as they would receive our friends, because of Christ. The Lord did have an Erastus in that city who made herself known to our daughter in an Uber ride. The connection was made as they talked in the ride about legal matters and then figured out that the other was a believer. The social identity as lawyers led to conversation that fostered a friendship among two believers.

Embracing Means: Trusting the Work of God through Us to Fulfill the Gospel

Rom 16:25–27

The oldest manuscripts do not contain verse 24, and scholars acknowledge this with notations in study and reference Bibles rather than acting as if there is no dispute on the words of this text. But the manuscripts are in agreement with Paul's giving glory to God. Paul praises God for two things: 1) that God is able to strengthen (or establish) believers through the gospel, and 2) that he is the wise God who intends to bring about the obedience of faith that comes from the gospel.

How does God strengthen us? Through the preaching of the mystery of the gospel, which, in Romans 11, concerns the partial hardening of Israel so that gentiles might come to faith. Through the first-century, large-scale rejection of Jesus, the gospel went from Jerusalem to non-Jewish soils all over Europe and Asia. In doing so, God's plan for all peoples to hear the gospel was being fulfilled. People from every society and all aspects of every society are those the gospel intends to bring into the church. Every church should be a welcome center for any and all believers, even as we pray, hope, give, and send missionaries so that people around the globe might know Christ in mercy.

Many evangelical churches have histories of being missions-minded with respect to global missions, even when they have missed matters of racial injustice in their own backyards. Like my church, an evangelical church might have the ubiquitous wall of missionaries and their prayer letters and participate in several strategic missions partnerships locally and internationally.

What are churches saying as they support the work of missions and their missions partners and as their members share faith in Christ with unbelievers in their spheres of influence? They—we—are telling everyone in all walks of life that there is a God who sent his Son so that he might embrace those sinners who would trust the Son and that we are evidence of that God in the way we embrace all people as we preach the message of Christ to them. We are inviting people to be embraced by Jesus, the one who redeems people from every tribe, nation, language, and land, through his death on the cross for sin and his powerful resurrection from the dead to offer life to those who believe on him.

CONCLUSION

Therefore, let us refrain from saying that our calling and identities are about souls only. If we do, our motives will be in question as we ignore the concern for whole persons, their practices, and their roles in society. Instead, let us look upon one another as *people*—beings whose entire makeup we should embrace, rather than invisible Tod Cliftons who soon can be forgotten. Acknowledging the dignity of full individuals is the beginning of scattering prejustice seeds in society. The hope is that the resulting fruit will bring justice for image-bearers of all genders and ethnicities, so that God's name will be known among all peoples of the world.

Bibliography

Asare, Janice Gassam. "Gender Equity Is Useless without Racial Equity." *Forbes*, 7 Mar 2020. https://www.forbes.com/sites/janicegassam/2020/03/07/gender-equity-is-useless-without-racial-equity/?sh=376c4cad7b4f.

Barr, Beth Allison. *The Making of Biblical Womanhood: How the Subjugation of Women Became Gospel Truth*. Grand Rapids: Brazos, 2021.

Burer, Michael H., and Daniel B. Wallace. "Was Junia Really an Apostle? A Re-examination of Rom 16.7." *New Testament Studies* 47 (2001) 76–91.

Burk, Denny. "Junia Is a Woman, and I Am a Complementarian." *Denny Burk* (blog), 8 Dec 2011. http://www.dennyburk.com/junia-is-a-woman-and-i-am-a-complementarian.

Byrd, Aimee. *Recovering from Biblical Manhood and Womanhood: How the Church Needs to Rediscover Her Purpose*. Grand Rapids: Zondervan, 2020.

Code Switch. "A Decade of Watching Black People Die." *NPR*, 31 May 2020. https://www.npr.org/2020/05/29/865261916/a-decade-of-watching-black-people-die.

Du Mez, Kristin Kobes. *Jesus and John Wayne: How White Evangelicals Corrupted a Faith and Fractured a Nation*. New York: Liveright, 2021.

Ellens, Cherita, and Felicia Davis. "The Intersection of Gender and Racial Equity: Why American Feminism Should Care." *Women Employed*, 6 Aug 2020. https://womenemployed.medium.com/the-intersection-of-gender-and-racial-equity-why-american-feminism-should-care-11af5d68164b.

Ellison, Ralph. *Invisible Man*. New York: Signet, 1952.

Entralgo, Rebekah. "The Eviction Crisis Is a Race and Gender Wage Gap Issue." *Inequality*, 6 Aug 2021. https://inequality.org/great-divide/cori-bush-eviction-wage-gap.

Fadel, Leila. "With Racial Attacks on the Rise, Asian Americans Fear for Their Safety." *NPR*, 22 Oct 2021. https://www.npr.org/sections/health-shots/2021/10/13/1045746655/1-in-4-asian-americans-recently-feared-their-household-being-targeted-poll-finds.

Frye, Jocelyn. "Racism and Sexism Combine to Shortchange Working Black Women." *Center for American Progress*, 22 Aug 2019. https://www.americanprogress.org/article/racism-sexism-combine-shortchange-working-black-women/.

Itkowitz, Colby. "Trump Again Uses Racially Insensitive Term to Describe Coronavirus." *Washington Post*, 23 June 2020. https://www.washingtonpost.com/politics/trump-again-uses-kung-flu-to-describe-coronavirus/2020/06/23/0ab5a8d8-b5a9-11ea-aca5-ebb63d27e1ff_story.html.

Li, Peggy. "Recent Developments Hitting the Ceiling: An Examination of Barriers to Success for Asian American Women." *Berkeley Journal of Gender, Law & Justice* 29 (2014) 140–67.

Moo, Douglas J. *The Epistle to the Romans*. Grand Rapids: Eerdmans, 1996.

The New Yorker. "Kadir Nelson's 'Say Their Names.'" *The New Yorker*, 14 June 2020. https://www.newyorker.com/culture/cover-story/cover-story-2020-06-22.

Patel, Pragna. "Notes on Gender and Racial Discrimination: An Urgent Need to Integrate an Intersectional Perspective to the Examination and Development of Policies,

Strategies and Remedies for Gender and Racial Equality." *United Nations*. https://www.un.org/womenwatch/daw/csw/Patel45.htm.

Petri, Alexandra E., and Daniel E. Slotnik. "Attacks on Asian-Americans in New York Stoke Fear, Anxiety and Anger." *The New York Times*, 26 Feb 2021. https://www.nytimes.com/2021/02/26/nyregion/asian-hate-crimes-attacks-ny.html.

Schreiner, Thomas R. *Romans*. 2nd ed. Grand Rapids: Baker, 2018.

Stenschke, C. W. "'Your Obedience Is Known to All' (Rom 16:19): Paul's References to Other Christians and Their Function in Paul's Letter to the Romans." *NovT* 57 (2015) 251–74.

Yam, Kimmy. "Trump Can't Claim 'Kung Flu' Doesn't Affect Asian Americans in This Climate, Experts Say." *NBC News*, 22 June 2020. https://www.nbcnews.com/news/asian-america/trump-can-t-claim-kung-flu-doesn-t-affect-asian-n1231812.

Zhou, Li. "Trump's Racist References to the Coronavirus Are His Latest Effort to Stoke Xenophobia." *Vox*, 23 June 2020. https://www.vox.com/2020/6/23/21300332/trump-coronavirus-racism-asian-americans.

Part Two

ECCLESIAL THEOLOGY

5

Race and the Opportunities of a Good News Witness

Vincent Bacote

I BEGIN WITH AN invitation to the reader. I have discovered that one of the challenges of addressing the topic of race is that it is easy to find oneself quickly taking a defensive posture in anticipation of facing information that is challenging or with which one disagrees. Many have had experiences where little constructive conversation occurs, because the temperature of the conversation quickly rises, and assertions are exchanged back and forth. Little if any understanding is the result of such situations, and preparing oneself for battle may seem necessary. My invitation asks each of us to take another stance, where we have a "tell me more" instead of a "yeah, but . . ." disposition. Whereas "yeah, but . . ." is more characteristic of preparing for defense and often suggests one has no interest in learning beyond settled opinion, "tell me more" does not require agreement but creates a setting for learning and sorting out what one reads or hears in conversations about race (or any other topic). I invite you to read on, consider your questions of clarification and points of disagreement, and imagine a path of constructive conversation that could occur after reading this chapter.

The Aim: A Good News Theology and Good News Ethics

Whether in conversation with pastor theologians or laypersons in the church, it is important to consider how our theology translates into life. If we are to engage the matter of racial justice, it is vital to do so out of life with God. While this seems pretty straightforward, the truth is that we have to face challenges to our theology. Consider the following common circumstance.

When people in evangelical communities say they have come to a place of dissonance with what was advertised as a good news theology, often they are saying the problem is more than what is proclaimed. They are speaking about a problem with the practice of Christianity that emerges from it. Dante Stewart's narrative provides a vivid example:

> After graduating from college, I joined a white evangelical church and entered seminary in the hopes of becoming a pastor there. In my pursuit to be a better person and a better athlete and a better Christian, I viewed Black sermons and Black songs and Black buildings and Black shouting and Black loving with skepticism and white sermons and white songs and white buildings and white clapping with sacredness.[1]

Before long, Stewart found himself in a crisis. He was in a church culture that seemed to require the denigration of Black culture and Black life, a crisis felt with greatest intensity when those in his church could not or would not understand his distress at the police shootings of men like Philando Castile and Alton Sterling. Black humanity itself seemed to be denied or disregarded. The distress became so great, he had to seek a survival strategy.

For Stewart, survival came by reading Black theologians such as James Cone, J. Deotis Roberts, and Stacey Floyd-Thomas, as well as immersing himself in Black poetry, music, and art. Reading the Bible differently and soaking in Black culture, Stewart found a fundamental dignity and love in the embrace and expression of Black culture. For him, this led to a liberation from a Jesus held captive by white religion. He concludes:

> My world changed when I stopped sitting at the feet of white Jesus and began becoming a disciple of Black Jesus. *I didn't have to hate myself or my people or our creativity or our beauty to be human or to be Christian.*[2]

This new world was not understood by those in the white evangelical culture Stewart had inhabited. What he found to be survival was regarded as walking

1. Stewart, "How I Learned," par. 3.
2. Stewart, "How I Learned," par. 19; italics added.

away from Jesus. Stewart's narrative conveys considerable dissonance. He vividly shows us the crisis he experienced in a setting where gospel proclamation was in tension with the affirmation of his *entire* humanness.

A similar example comes from my colleague Dr. Jordan Ryan:

> "I thought that Filipinos couldn't be professors here."
>
> It was my first week as a full-time college educator. Less than two months out of my PhD, I was nervous and excited to be teaching at Wheaton College, a Christian liberal arts college. Excited to impact the lives of students, but nervous because I was green and freshly arrived in the United States from Canada. My introductory New Testament class had just let out, so the room was empty except for one student who stood before me. His skin was brown like mine.
>
> "What, at Wheaton?" I asked, with a wry smile. I thought I knew where this was going.
>
> "No. In America."
>
> I felt his words run through me like electricity, shocking me, striking deep. Years later, they still reverberate through me.
>
> I got to know that student better over the course of the year. He had never seen a Filipino person like him or like me in an academic role in the US. It was even more surprising to him that I was in the role of someone who taught the Bible, a position usually filled by white westerners, both in the US diaspora and the Philippines.

Later in the article, he reflects further:

> The first time that I realized that the Church had failed me was when, at fifteen years old, my family was invited to lunch on a Sunday after service by a worship leader, who I had seen as a mentor, and his wife. Since I was a musician and rookie worship leader myself, my family believed that the invitation extended out of that mentor-mentee relationship. We quickly discovered that the purpose of the invitation was for this couple to ask my mother if any of her sisters could serve as a nanny to their children. It was deeply wounding for my family and led me to realize that we were being racialized in a way that was deeply harmful, but that I did not fully yet understand.[3]

Ryan conveys the difficulties of internalized inferiority (seen in his student) and presumed servitude (seen in the couple). Here we see a dissonance with

---

3. Ryan, "Underclass Myth," paras. 1–6, 11.

evangelical forms of faith that may have proclaimed equality of persons before God but left in place hierarchies based on ethnicity and class.

The experiences of Stewart and Ryan are not unique. Others have their own narratives, but the common thread is that of encountering a theology presented as faithful to the Bible, as an expression of the good news, only to be ethically expressed in ways that are found to be limited at best and harmful at worst.

A WAY FORWARD?

In the cases above, most notably for Stewart, a fuller encounter with the good news comes by taking paths besides those paved by Evangelicals. Reading widely is important, as no Christian tradition is the exclusive domain of truth. As an Evangelical who reads these narratives and who has heard similar stories, I am prompted to ask, "Is it *necessary* to take the path of racial or ethnic contextual theologies to faithfully proclaim and practice the good news?" The point of the question is not to challenge the validity of these versions of contextual theology (and I hasten to add that evangelical theology is also contextual, even as it aims for a theology of complete fidelity to the Bible without being contextually determined). The question is whether evangelical theology has deficiencies and lacunae/blind spots that make it perpetually unable to convey (in practice) the good news of the gospel in ways that humanize and elevate all persons. Must Stewart, Ryan, and others turn elsewhere to experience proclamation and practice that affirms their full humanity?

My answer: I don't think so.

Before I further explain my answer, we have to ask: What hasn't happened that might have enabled the utilization of the broader tradition? What has been missing in "good news" spaces that has led some to make an exit or at least to take a hiatus from these spaces for the sake of sanity and wholeness? What has happened (and keeps happening) that has led Stewart and others to conclude that inhabiting American white evangelical spaces results in antagonism to nonwhite ethnic identities (and, arguably, perhaps most intensely to anti-Blackness)?

I am aware that some progress has been made. We are not where we were, and amid the frustrations about topics such as nationalism and arguments about critical race theory, there are those who are actively seeking ways to face and engage these challenges on the question of race.[4] Of course, this is

---

4. One very obvious example: the fact that there was a controversy of Resolution 9 regarding critical race theory and intersectionality at the 2019 Southern Baptist Convention is itself evidence that there is not only antagonism toward questions of race (see "On

positive news, so it is less likely to go viral. But let us make no mistake: we are far from something like a revival on issues such as racial justice, and churches in the majority culture are not known for leading the way in such things. But we still have the opportunity. What needs to happen for our theology to be good news for all?[5]

GLIMPSES OF GOOD NEWS?

Below, I invite us to consider three examples of how our theology and doctrine might provide glimpses of the good news in proclamation and practice. Specifically, I am considering how dimensions of evangelical theology can be expressed in ways that are good news to some of the challenges of race.

Considering Our Ecclesiology

I begin with our ecclesiology, particularly with a focus on 1 Cor 12:14–27. Those of evangelical background who read this have most likely heard numerous sermons on this text where Paul emphasizes the truth that all members of the church are necessary, using the metaphor of the body. He tells the Corinthian church (and us) that every Christian has received spiritual gifts from God and emphasizes our unity as one body.

While there are many avenues to take with this text, I propose a few that could be expressions of the good news in evangelical settings. First, there is the place of *diversity and generosity*. Many of us have been part of conversations with fellow Christians about spiritual gifts, including discussion about how to create space for the variety of gifts rather than a magnification of some and a diminishment of others. When we consider addressing the challenges of race, here I wish to emphasize the importance of the variety of approaches and strategies used by different members of the body. For example, there are those who describe the complex questions and dynamics of race, those who analyze the dynamics and strive to explain how race has emerged and continues to function in our world, and those who are prophetic and urge us to see how racial injustices are an offense to God. There are those who focus on the church,

---

Critical Race Theory"). It required more than ethnic minorities in order to be successful. The loud opposition reveals reasons for great concern, but the existence of opposition does not mean there has not been any progress. This is only one example, but the important point is that lots of attention to opposition should not lead to the conclusion that there has been no progress. Of course, the opposite is true: the fact of progress in no way means the marathon is close to the end.

5. I discuss this in Bacote, *Reckoning with Race.*

those who focus on politics and public policy, and those who focus on other matters of culture. There is overlap, of course, but the point is that there are many areas of emphasis, and we need to equip and encourage the members of the body in their areas of emphasis without creating unnecessary competition. A dynamic that sometimes occurs (on this issue and others) is that the emphasis of one person, group, or ministry can be so well and urgently expressed that it suggests that it is the only area of need. Urgency is understandable, but it need not create the false impression of a limited scope of mission on questions of race or anything else. To convey the good news in the face of the challenges of race, we need the full scope of gifts/emphases in the church and a disposition of generosity to those with other strategies.

A second expression of the good news relates to verse 26. There we see the important emphasis that the community should be characterized not by competition but rather *empathy and celebration*: "If one part suffers, every part suffers with it; if one part is honored, every part rejoices with it" (NIV). While many sermons in evangelical churches may highlight empathy with suffering and celebration of the gifts of others, there is a further important emphasis relevant to distress experienced by many minorities in evangelical spaces. This text invites us to practice empathy and to consider ways to share in the suffering of those who have experienced hurt and trauma connected with race (as vividly expressed above by Stewart and Ryan). There are basic pastoral care questions here: Is there care for these traumatized and hurting members of the body? If one of our members suffers, do we really suffer with them? Or do we tell them, "We will let you know when you are suffering?" Do we practice this dimension of loving our neighbors as ourselves?

How might such care be needed? Care is needed, for example, just from contending with the avalanche of exposure to racial trauma. While there are positive benefits from the perpetual news cycle of the communications revolution, and while social media applications have potentially made everyone a news reporter, the negative effects can be great when one encounters the horrors of racial antagonism again and again. The aim of "letting people know" about racial offenses can easily become harmful in a way analogous to being in a war. Just as a person exposed to battle can experience post-traumatic stress disorder, the experience of a steady stream of horrible incidents can be overwhelming and traumatic. Care is also needed for those with experiences of racial hostility. If a member of your church has experienced racial hostility, what is your response? How do you enter into their suffering and (if possible) help them gain justice and healing? How do you care for those bewildered and confused because they are not sure what to do when they are at first excited about their experience in evangelical communities but then find themselves in circumstances like those above? All of this brings us to the big question: Do we take care of the body and empathize with the whole body, or do we give honor and care only to some parts and not others? In evangelical contexts, is the church a good news community in proclamation and practice for everyone? If Evangelicals are truly "people of the book," I think the answer can be in the affirmative, but the jury is still out.

Considering Our Anthropology

A second area of theology and doctrine is our theological anthropology, our doctrine of humanity. Who do we say we are? What goes unspoken in the way we speak about our common humanity? For evangelical leaders: in your church, how do people understand themselves as humans made in the image of God? Do they mainly regard themselves as sinful humans as a result of the fall? Do they view themselves as those who were born sinners but are now redeemed children of God? Where in the midst of this kind of standard language do we take for granted certain aspects of what it means to be seen as a full human being? What occurs in evangelical churches proclaiming our common humanity that yet somehow leads the Dante Stewarts and Jordan Ryans to experience themselves as not quite as fully human as those in the majority culture?

There is a big challenge here: How do we give affirmation to our particularity without turning the good of our cultural particularity into subterranean idolatries of "our people" and implicit or explicit condescension toward "others," particularly racial/ethnic others? It is no solution to replace white supremacy with any other idolatrous ethnic supremacy; but a docetic[6] anthropology clothed in language of "common humanity" will not suffice either. It is a great irony to confess "we share a common humanity" while denying some or all of the characteristics that go into the expression of our lived humanness in times, places, with language and food and clothing and customs. Much can go unsaid that is prominent and apparent in the way one understands what it is to be a human. Our common humanity is clothed with our culture, and we can resist the temptation to purportedly deny cultural particularities (while actually taking ours for granted) while affirming what we share as humans. We can admit we have culture in the same manner we can admit we are flesh and blood.

6. Docetism is a christological heresy that denies the humanity of Christ. To be docetic in our anthropology is to deny the characteristics that make us human. While this includes embodiment, it also includes how we conduct our lives in times and places as embodied persons.

When our cultural particularities are brought under the lordship of Christ, changes will likely occur, but this is not cultural erasure as much as cultural refinement. The gifts of our various cultures can be treasured without being worshipped. This is not a path toward the elevation of one culture over another in a kind of cultural Olympics games, but instead the opportunity to bring glory to God, as we see in Rev 7:9. The multitude is there praising God in the beauty of their cultural particularity even as the Lord is the singular focus of worship. Does your anthropology (and mine) have space for seeking out and rooting out the idols of culture without succumbing to the falsehood of docetism? How might our strategies of Christian formation help us to give gratitude and glory to God for the cultural gifts of his entire creation and not only our local flavors?

Considering Our Sanctification

Sanctification is a doctrine that ought to lend itself to an easy marriage of theology and ethics. In 1 Cor 1:2, Paul addresses the Corinthians as those who have an identity as God's holy people and as those who are called to pursue a path of living up to and into that identity. Sanctification is a matter of what is true about us simply because we belong to God, as well as what we hope to become more true of us as we grow in likeness to Christ. My point here is not to get into debates about the level of change Christians can expect but to invite us to consider how best to convey that part of the good news in our ongoing transformation as a result of the work of the Holy Spirit in the lives of God's people. The progressive dimension of sanctification is one of the ways we experience within ourselves foretastes of our future experience as completely transformed humans. To be sanctified in fullness is to be made more fully and properly human, a transformation that will make us into people who give glory to God in our worship of him and in our disposition toward our fellow human beings.

What might sanctification look like as we contend with racial injustice? I will briefly suggest some ways of engaging challenges of race as part of an openness to the Spirit's transformative work in the sanctification process. Perhaps one of the first aspects of the sanctification process is to give us a proper disposition of courage and peace instead of fear. It is likely the case that many Christians are uncertain what to do in the face of questions of race. The Spirit's work may lead us away from the conspiracy of silence that can result from fear regarding discussion of issues of race. Minorities may be fearful and speak up only out of a need to survive; those in the majority may be hesitant to speak up, recognizing their own uncertainty about the issues involved and fearing an emotional explosion (for certain, the latter sometimes occurs when people have long-held frustrations). This impasse requires moving beyond fear and into courage for all involved, because there is great potential for misunderstanding and likely moments of deep frustration. The only way forward, however, is to enter this dense aspect of our life together as God's people, acknowledging fears and seeking courage from the Lord.

A second expression of sanctification can be welcoming a transformed vision of others and a pursuit of one's vocation in addressing race. The distortion field of sin can easily lead us to regard others in partial and/or wrong ways, and it is easy for any of us to become settled in our understanding of others. Sanctification can lead us to humility about the limitations of our perception and orient us toward curiosity (rather than certainty) about those different from us. In addition, openness to the Spirit can prompt us to consider how the pursuit of racial justice is an aspect of God's vocation for each of us (instead of an area of special interest for some).

Third, our sanctification can give us a disposition of holy patience and impatience. In the same way we need patience as we long for the fullness of God's kingdom to arrive, we need patience amid the long process of engaging and pursuing racial justice. Along with this, a holy impatience is necessary as one part of helping us press forward (without confusing our pursuit of justice with bringing the fullness of God's kingdom).

Fourth, our sanctification ought to include an openness to and desire for the necessary transformation of character. As with any type of change we want to see in the world, we need to not only think about the change that happens "out there" but also consider the changes needed within us, so that we are open to the ways God wishes to make us more Christlike (do we need more humility, more patience, more generosity toward others, etc.?).

And finally, our openness to sanctification can help yield a perspective that does not limit God to bringing justice through our systems alone. Even the best imaginable strategies for public policy or cultural renewal are subject to revision. They are public experiments that we hope will enable a more just world. A lens of sanctification should lead us to humbly propose strategies and do our best while waiting for God to bring about the ultimate justice.

Conclusion

Ecclesiology, anthropology, and sanctification are merely examples of doctrines that could be expressed in evangelical spaces in ways that open paths of flourishing to all. Of course, each church has a tradition. Each church has a statement of beliefs. Evangelicals need to consider how these beliefs lead to or connect to Christian practice. How are the people in our churches putting into practice those beliefs? How are those beliefs expressed in ways that address the challenge of race? Are they leading to glimpses of the kingdom that is coming? While I empathize and understand the frustrations expressed by many who feel they must depart evangelical spaces in order to flourish as more fully human people, I continue to believe it is possible that evangelical churches and institutions contain the potential to humanize everyone. In order for this to be more than my hopeful words, evangelical leaders need to consider how the beliefs of their traditions show that the good news of God's kingdom is not less than our proclamation but is definitely more than words.

Bibliography

Bacote, Vincent. *Reckoning with Race and Performing the Good News: In Search of a Better Evangelical Theology*. Leiden: Brill, 2020.

"On Critical Race Theory and Intersectionality." *Southern Baptist Convention*, 1 June 2019. https://www.sbc.net/resource-library/resolutions/on-critical-race-theory-and-intersectionality/.

Ryan (Cruz), Jordan J. "The Underclass Myth and Taking Our Rightful Place at the Foot of the Table." *Asian American Christian Collaborative*, 12 Oct 2021. https://www.asianamericanchristiancollaborative.com/article/the-underclass-myth-and-taking-our-rightful-place-at-the-foot-of-the-table.

Stewart, Dante. "How I Learned That Jesus Is Black." *The New York Times*, 16 Oct 2021. https://www.nytimes.com/2021/10/16/opinion/jesus-black-james-cone.html.

6

Pursuing Racial Solidarity
as the Local Church

MICHELLE AMI REYES

MOST OF US KNOW a pastor whose words on issues of race make us cringe. That one pastor who is quick to offer insensitive commentary, whether it be from the pulpit or in communal life, outside the four walls of the church. In my life, I've known many, but there is one pastor in particular whose views and words are an apt reflection of the abrasive sentiments that certain conservative evangelical leaders espouse. I will call him Joe. Joe is a white pastor, and he was hard to talk to. The minute I would start sharing about my own personal life and experiences as a brown-skinned woman or of racial tragedies in our country at large, Joe would immediately become restless. His fingers became fidgety, his body would shift dramatically, and his eyes sometimes rolled whenever I said words like "racism" or "hurting." He made each word that came from my mouth feel like an annoyance to him, and more often than not, before I could even finish my statement, he would interject, wanting to tell me as quickly and vehemently as he could that the experiences I was relating to him about racialized minorities in the United States were in fact false.

I didn't even have to be having a conversation on race with Joe in order to suddenly find myself dragged into a convoluted racial debate. We would be talking about the new shoes somebody was wearing (which happened to be white), and then suddenly Joe would make a joke about how when you're white, you stick out and people hate you, and then follow that with a line about how he teaches his congregation to share the gospel of Jesus with nonbelievers without bowing to the idols of racism. Joe had a unique talent of weaving any topic—from sports to food—into an issue of white people being lied to by Black and Brown folks who were just playing the victim card and trying to take advantage of him. Joe's theological views usually intersected with *Fox News* talking points and the idea that racism had already been cured in the sixties. He was pretty sure that the core doctrines of the Christian faith and even the rhythms of communal life together for the church were in jeopardy because of too much focus on the "lies" of race today. His solution was to stop talking about race and just focus on the gospel.

Prior to 2020, it was hard enough to simply tolerate Joe. He seemed to come to every network gathering ready for a fight. He never showed interest in hearing anyone's opinion other than his own. In his mind, he was always right. In short, Joe was not interested in talking about any issues—race or otherwise—that didn't impact him or his specific congregation personally. If it wasn't impacting his day-to-day life, then it wasn't his problem. And if he wasn't experiencing it, he assumed the problem really didn't exist.

To be honest, I was never interested in trying to win an intellectual debate with Joe. What I was looking for was racial solidarity. At its most basic level, gospel-rooted racial solidarity means showing up and standing up for a person or group whose plight might not appear to have anything to do with one's own. I simply wanted Joe to see me and to care about what I was going through and what my community was going through. But Joe was incapable of expressing empathy, let alone lament, for the pains I had experienced in my life. Instead, when we talked about race issues, it seemed like his sole objective was to deny these experiences. Over time, I felt less inclined to engage Joe in conversation. The anger that rose inside of me and the words I wanted to shout back were harder and harder to suppress. I learned that sometimes the best way to love Joe was not to talk to Joe.

Then the murder of George Floyd happened on May 25, 2020, and Joe became radicalized. He began to believe that people who spouted "false realities" about race should be labeled heretics. All of a sudden, Joe and I were no longer two Christians, one white, one Brown, seeing and experiencing the world in different ways. Now he was the Christ-follower, and I the Marxist. He was the keeper of orthodoxy, and I, a Jezebel. There was no longer space for me at the table to share stories about hurting communities. When I was around Joe, my whole energy and time became redirected toward simply *proving* I was a Christian. Unsurprisingly, it wasn't long before there was a complete breakdown of our relationship. In Joe's mind, I was no longer part of the body of Christ and thus no longer someone worth even addressing.

Sadly, this is the formula that many Christians of color experience when trying to seek racial solidarity for themselves personally and in the church. First, their stories are dismissed; then, their theology and worldview are questioned; and, finally, their personhood is delegitimized and rejected. So often, Christians of color just want to be heard and understood. We want people to mourn with us, but too often, the response is simply "heretic, get out."

THE PROBLEM OF MORAL PROXIMITY

When it comes to the issue of race in the church today, the body of Christ is experiencing a familial crisis. Instead of embracing each other as brothers and sisters who bear each other's burdens (Gal 6:2), we treat each other more like the crazy uncle that needs to be disinvited to the holiday dinner and avoided at all costs. Families are supposed to have each other's backs, no matter what. Brothers and sisters are supposed to look out for each other when no one else does. But that's not what we see happening with brothers and sisters of different ethnicities in the church. Quite the opposite, in fact. Many Black, Brown, and white Christians don't know how to show up and stand up for each other. We much prefer to shame, insult, and reject as opposed to embrace, love, and protect. Our family in the church is in shambles.

There are many reasons why Black, Brown, and white Christians have a hard time caring about each other's racialized experiences of pain. Barna data shows that in our post-2020 world, some Christians simply feel "unmotivated" (12 percent) or "not at all motivated" (16 percent) to address racial injustice and inequity in the United States.[1] Part of the reason for this lack of motivation stems from the paralyzing weight of US racial history. Many folks think, "I don't know where to start, so I won't start anywhere." Lack of personal relationships also stymies motivation. I've heard many churches say something to the effect of "well, we don't know anybody in those communities, so we don't know where to send support." Sometimes, white Christians don't believe they can ever fully know the true depths of the Black experience in the US, or the Asian American, Latino, or Native American experience, for that matter, and this line of reasoning also becomes a justification for sidelining themselves.

1. "White Christians Have Become," para. 7.

Racial solidarity isn't just lacking in white churches, though. It's also absent in Brown and Black churches. For example, since March 2020, the Stop AAPI Hate reporting center has catalogued over 9,000 incidents of anti-Asian hate crimes.[2] I was deeply encouraged by Dr. Jarvis Williams's admonition that "redemptive kingdom diversity calls for ethnically diverse people of God to stand in solidarity with our Asian American neighbors against anti-Asian racism."[3] However, not every Black, Latino, or Native American church has called out the sin of anti-Asian racism over this past year or lamented the death of the six Asian women murdered in Atlanta on March 16, 2021. Likewise, not every Asian church speaks up for the dignity of Black lives. Many Asian churches were silent in the aftermath of the murders of Eric Garner, Michael Brown, Ahmaud Arbery, and Breonna Taylor. Not every Black church takes an interest in the issues of immigration at the US southern border. Not every Black church spoke up after the murder of twenty-three people in a Walmart in El Paso on August 3, 2019, or the crisis of Haitian migrants under the Del Rio International Bridge in Texas in September 2021. Not every Latino church speaks up about missing indigenous women and children. Sometimes the reasoning goes, "We can't identify with that issue. We're just outsiders." But more often than not, a minority church cares more about its own issues because it has believed the lie of a scarcity mentality. We think there is not enough time, energy, resources, or space for everyone's griefs and pains to be treated equally, side by side. We all feel like our own house is burning. How are we supposed to care for other people's burning houses right now too?

Threaded through each of these reasons is a common denominator: self-preservation, which is ultimately rooted in selfishness. Much of our unhealthy and unproductive engagement as Christians today around racial solidarity as majority and minority cultures stems from our inability to see outside of our own life and perspective. Pastor Clark Fobes argues,

> Our failure to compassionately care for [others] is not a sign of our biblical convictions, but our own inability to identify with and extend Gospel love to those outside of our purview. The problem lies not with those other "undeserving" groups, but with us. . . . In ethics and moral philosophy, there is a common principle of moral proximity that leads to moral obligation: if I am relationally more proximate to one person or group over another, then I am more morally obligated to helping their cause than the other. . . . The problem with the principle of moral proximity, however, (as pointed out by many modern philosophers) is that it never leads

2. Yellow Horse et al., "Stop AAPI Hate."

3. Williams, *Redemptive Kingdom Diversity*, 159.

us to care for those beyond our own confines. This means we never feel obligated to care about those different from us—whether geographically, racially, socially, familial, and the like.[4]

We also don't want to talk about the issues that people different from us are experiencing. A study of 2006 portraits of American life revealed shocking disparities in racial understanding, with 43 percent of whites saying one of the most effective ways to improve race relations is to stop talking about race.[5] By 2012, 55 percent of whites wanted to stop talking about race.[6] Too often, the preferred response to problems of racial pain is "don't ask, don't tell." People assume that if they stop talking about the problems of race that *other people are experiencing*, they'll go away on their own.

However, a healthy family shouldn't avoid each other's pains. When you love your brother or sister, you don't brush their problems under the rug and hope they go away. You're not supposed to just stop talking to your parent or relative because they're hurting or tell them that they can't come over and hang out until they get their business sorted out. We don't tell family, "Sorry, I've got my own problems I'm dealing with. Leave me alone and deal with your own issues by yourself." No, we're supposed to sit with each other in our pain. We're supposed to hug each other, cry with each other, take care of the other person, make sure they get food and water and sleep, lend them money if they need it, or offer them our couch to sleep on. We show up. We say, "Are you OK?" "How can I help you?" and "Have you eaten?" Then we show up again and again and again—because that's what family does. Even if our sibling lives halfway across the country, we don't distance ourselves from him or her. We draw near. We get in the mess, and we figure it out together.

A CREED OF ONENESS

If we want to grow in our ability to pursue racial solidarity as a church, we must build deep, familial bonds with Christians of other ethnicities and cultures. This is, in fact, the apostle Paul's charge to the church in Galatia. In Gal 3:26–29, Paul writes: "So in Christ Jesus you are all children of God through faith, for all of you who were baptized into Christ have clothed yourselves with Christ. There is neither Jew nor Gentile, neither slave nor free, nor is there male and female, for you are all one in Christ Jesus. If you belong to Christ, then you are Abraham's seed, and heirs according to the promise" (NIV). Paul

4. Fobes, "Privilege of Single-Issue Voting," para. 9.

5. Emerson and Sikkink, "Portraits of American Life Study, 1st Wave."

6. Emerson and Sikkink, "Portraits of American Life Study, 2nd Wave."

writes these words to an ethnically divided church. The believers in Galatia had been drawing stark lines in the sand for who were considered brothers and sisters in Christ and who were not. There was a faction of Jewish believers in the Galatian church who insisted that gentile converts accept the Jewish law, e.g., adhere to circumcision, if they were to belong to God's people. The resulting chaos and exclusion that these demands brought created a crisis of family within the Galatian church.

Paul steps into this messy familial situation and argues that because gentile converts have embraced Christ and received the Spirit just like Jewish believers, they are no less full heirs of Israel's promises. He counters the Galatians' false claims of family with an eschatological vision of unity and equality in Christ. In Gal 3:26, Paul declares that all believers are God's children. No matter if they are Greek or Jew, slave or free, man or woman—each person in Christ is a full member of God's people, because, as Dr. Craig Keener outlines, they are: 1) baptized (initiated) into Christ (3:27a); 2) clothed with Christ (3:27b); 3) corporately one in Christ (3:28); 4) Abraham's offspring (3:29a); and thus 5) heirs of the coming world together according to the promise (3:29b).[7] What Paul creates in this passage is a utopic picture, an ideal, in which nothing divides us—not language or ethnicity, not gender or customs, not socioeconomic class or racialized experiences in the world—because we are all one in Christ. John Calvin writes in his commentary on Galatians, "Christ makes them all one. Whatever may have been their former differences, Christ alone is able to unite them all."[8] In other words, ethnic differences should no longer divide believers. Gentiles don't have to erase who they are to become children of God. Their voices and stories and experiences still matter and should be retained.[9] Paul's criticism in Gal 3:26–29 is of the Jews who were not treating fellow gentile believers the way brothers and sisters in the Lord should, namely, as equals and as one.

That being said, oneness should not be equated to sameness. Sameness isn't the goal for the christological family. Believers are not commanded to erase their ethnic identities or racialized experiences. Too often, Gal 3:26–29 is used as a justification to erase our social and cultural distinctives. Contrary to a surface-level reading of these verses, however, Paul is stressing in Galatians 3 and throughout his letters that we need to lean into these identities while learning how to enjoy and connect with those who are different from

7. Keener, *Galatians*, 937.

8. Calvin, *Epistles of Paul*, 69.

9. The *South Asia Bible Commentary* offers insightful application from Gal 3:26–28 in an eastern context for both class division and stigmatizing views against women (Wintle, *South Asia Bible Commentary*, 1624–25).

us.[10] As Dr. Eric Redmond argued at the Fall 2021 CPT conference, Scripture shows that "personhood with all of our positive social identifiers should be embraced for the glory of God."[11] In other words, followers of Jesus must see each person as a unique individual with their own distinct cultural identity and racialized experiences. We must understand that we are different from each other, and the world treats us in different ways; but despite that, we will go against the status quo to declare that our lives are interconnected. We will declare that, in Christ, our joys and pains and lives all intersect and that what impacts one of us, impacts all of us.

Drs. M. Sydney Park and Kenneth A. Matthews poignantly elucidate the application of reconciliation and integration from Gal 3:26–29 for modern Christians. They write that the good news of Galatians 3 means that

> we preach to all ethnic groups that have formerly been excluded. The Asian Christians should proclaim to the Hispanic Christians: "We are now reconciled and united in Christ Jesus!" The white Christians should proclaim to the black Christians: "There is now no enmity between races in Christ Jesus!" The Indian Christians should proclaim to the Hispanic Christians: "Because of the cross of Jesus Christ we are members of the same body!"[12]

We cannot interpret Gal 3:26–29 through a purely spiritual lens. Keener argues,

> One can hardly say that Galatians 3:28 addresses only salvation as if salvation itself lacks transformative implications for relationships. One cannot fully isolate 3:28 from relevance to social contexts since social conflict informs the entire letter. The already side of the "already not yet" tensions of the kingdom did impact social relationships between Jews and Gentiles (2:11–14) and slave and free (Phlm 16), men and women, including in marriage.[13]

Thomas Schreiner likewise argues that the solidarity principle in Galatians 3 speaks to sociocultural contexts. He explains that Gal 3:28 in particular means that "as coheirs of the promise of Abraham, Jews are not superior to

---

10. Cf. Paul's treatise in 1 Cor 9:19–23, in which he says, "I have become all things to all people so that by all possible means I might save some" (v. 22). I argue that in this passage, "Paul emphasizes cultural identities as part of the Christian faith and encourages Christians to respect cultural differences" (Reyes, *Becoming All Things*, 12); see also Hays's analysis on Gal 3:26–29 (*From Every People*, 182–87).

11. Redmond, "Embracing the Other."

12. Matthews and Park, *Post-Racial Church*, 211.

13. Keener, *Galatians*, 947.

gentiles, those who are free are not more important than slaves, and men are not worth more than women. All those who are united to Christ are equal as members of Abraham's family."[14] Paul doesn't rule out the existence of the distinct and identifiable social groups listed in Gal 3:26–29; rather, he argues that there should be equality among each people and group. The language of us being "all children of God" should thus not simplistically be interpreted as recipients of spiritual blessings in Christ through faith but, rather, as a complex declaration of physical, social, and cultural solidarity.

Gal 3:26–28 creates the foundation for a solidarity ethic in the church. Instead of conforming to the pattern of the world that draws a line between us and them, the church should take a different posture: there should be *no* us, *no* them. There should be only we. Ethnicity, class, gender—these things should no longer be used to insulate people from each other. And not just our cultural expressions, but our racialized experiences of pain should each be treated equally. A man should care about the pains and struggles that a woman has, an African American should care about the pains and struggles that a Latino has, an Anglo-American should care about the pains and struggles that an Asian American has, and so on.

Moreover, the solidarity ethic of Gal 3:26–29 should completely disrupt the world's way of defining moral obligation. We must intentionally and verbally declare that the Black Christians and the Latino Christians on the other side of town are "our brothers and sisters." We must intentionally and verbally declare that the Asian American and Native American Christians on the north side or the east side are "our brothers and sisters." We may not be physically proximate to each other, but as a family under the banner of Christ, we have an obligation of moral proximity to each other to physically and spiritually care for each other. Because when you're my brother or my sister, I will show up and stand up next to you when you're hurting. Your pain is my pain too.

Supposed Limits to Racial Solidarity

There are a few counter-responses I can anticipate to this concept of a solidarity ethic. "But wait," you might say, "certain issues don't impact our congregants personally. We're a predominantly white church, we don't have Asian Americans," or "We're a predominantly Black church, we don't have Latino immigrants," or "We're a predominantly Asian church, we don't have Native Americans." To which I would argue that the Galatian creed in 3:26–29 is not just for the local church, but it also extends to the big-*c* Church as well. For

14. Schreiner, *Galatians*, 258.

example, in the wake of the March 16 Atlanta massacre, even if you didn't have any Asian congregants in your church, did you reach out to a local Asian church and ask how you could lament and grieve together? In the wake of George Floyd's death, many Black churches held prayer vigils. Did you reach out to any local Black churches and ask if your church could join?

"But wait," you might say, "the solidarity ethic in Galatians 3 is about caring for fellow believers, not addressing the world at large. What about Galatians 6:10, for example, which states, 'Therefore, as we have opportunity, let us do good to all people, *especially* to those who belong to the family of believers?'" Some have used verses like this to argue that the church's priority should focus inward. "What if *our* congregants are hurting?" some ask. "Shouldn't we take care of our brothers and sisters in Christ first, those who are members of our specific congregation?" This thinking, however, creates a false dichotomy. It makes us believe that we can care only for ourselves or others, not both. But that is nothing more than a mentality of scarcity again. Gal 6:10, in fact, first emphasizes the need to do good to *all* people. This means that the church should never see it as a waste to care for non-Christians. In times of crisis (and in times of stability, for that matter) the body of Christ should open up its care, attention, and resources for the entire community. In the wake of a racial tragedy, for example, the entire community should know they can count on the local church and feel cared for by the church.

RACIAL SOLIDARITY IN MOTION

Before giving practical applications of what racial solidarity looks like, it's important to understand what racial solidarity is not and what it does not look like. Pursuing racial solidarity as a church is not the same thing as being multiethnic or even multicultural. Too often these terms are conflated, but they mean vastly different things. Multiethnic refers to a collection of more than one ethnic group in contrast to monoethnic (meaning only one ethnic group). Multicultural means the existence and equal treatment of different cultural values, ideas, and communication styles. Multicultural is a word that you might hear in conjunction with the idea of inclusion, such as having diverse leadership or offering bilingual or multilingual church services. Being multiethnic and multicultural should equate to different peoples of different cultures not only seeing their ethnicity and culture represented in leadership and on stage but also seeing, hearing, and engaging with their culture at church in other meaningful ways. They should be able to see their language reflected in worship, in the styles of songs and prayer. Being a multiethnic, multicultural church also means regularly eating together with different foods represented from different cultures. This kind of cultural representation is important. There are biblical precedents for this. But cultural representation is not the same as racial solidarity.

Racial solidarity is also not the same as racial reconciliation. Racial reconciliation at its core is helping people of different ethnicities and cultures get along. Sometimes this means acknowledging and atoning for wrongs done, asking for the victim's forgiveness, and resolving never to repeat the wrongs. But typically, racial reconciliation has an individual and interpersonal bent. The goal is getting people back together, to become friends and live life together. Racial solidarity goes beyond racial reconciliation.

Finally, racial solidarity is not necessarily political either. When we talk about biblically rooted racial solidarity, we are not talking about partisanship. Racial solidarity cannot be forced into conventional categories of political activity, especially because the goal of racial solidarity isn't to achieve identifiable policy victories.

Racial solidarity simply means caring about the issues threatening both your own congregation and the surrounding communities of color and working together toward solutions that are both just and equitable. We must reimagine what it means to live life together as the collective body and hold a robust understanding of partnerships with each other's plights and causes. As Dr. Anthony Bradley argues, white "evangelicals will need to learn now to partner and build relationships with predominantly minority denominations that share the same commitments to the gospel and the authority of Scripture."[15] A local church committed to pursuing racial solidarity will link arms with people of other ethnicities and cultures through both the highs and the lows of corporate life together. There are five practical ways we can begin doing this today.

1. Acknowledge Racial Pain and Tragedies from the Pulpit

The leadership of a church sets the tone for how racial pains and tragedies are addressed in communal life. Congregants need to hear from the pastor, elders, and staff that you see them. In the aftermath of a shooting or death, there can be so much comfort in the leadership telling brothers and sisters of color, "I'm so sorry for what happened. I'm grieving with you." Give them a hug. Pray for them in the pastoral prayer. Oftentimes after a local or national tragedy, our church scraps the sermon for that Sunday and writes a sermon specifically

---

15. Bradley, "General Introduction," 20.

tailored to the issue at hand. Make sure that racial pain and tragedies are addressed regularly from the pulpit.

2. Practice Corporate Lament

Create regular rhythms of lament in your church. For us, at Hope Community Church, this means hosting a monthly corporate prayer gathering with a designated time for lament. This gives opportunity for our brothers and sisters of color to express the hurt and the grief that they are shouldering. Moreover, it gives opportunity for other congregants to hear and engage up close with this pain. So much healing, as well as education and awareness, happens in this space. Corporate lament also teaches congregants that they can bring their specific racialized pains to God. Never underestimate the power of corporate lament.

3. Give Financially

As a church, ask yourself how you can give financially as an expression of racial solidarity. For congregants in your church struggling with mental health due to incidents of racism, can you allocate funds from your compassion fund to help with counseling and therapy? Could you allocate funds for your pastors and staff of color to have gym memberships or funds for counseling or even date nights with spouses to care for their holistic health in the aftermath of racial tragedies? After neighborhoods are looted or destroyed from riots, how can your church support local minority businesses? Our money speaks volumes to our commitment to holistically care for our Black and Brown family.

4. Engage in Marches, Walks, & Bike Rides

Last year, our church organized a march in partnership with our local Christian Community Development Association (CCDA) network around East Austin after the deaths of George Floyd, Breonna Taylor, and Mike Ramos. We did the march in silence. Some of us held signs. Most of us were just silently praying as we walked. But it was a powerful moment in our community, as it showed first and foremost to our local Black and Brown residents that the local church was standing with them. This is what marches, walks, and bike rides should accomplish. They should be declarations of peace-filled solidarity. Done well, they also raise awareness for those who do not yet know about the issue. These events don't have to be organized by the church. In fact, we should be open to joining other churches' and organizations' marches too. Solidarity means showing that we don't always have to be in charge.

5. Join Protests

Their are times when the church needs to engage in solidarity with a loud voice. At Hope Community Church, we have stood outside of the governor's mansion in Austin to protest the conviction of Rodney Reed on death row. Our church has joined Black churches across Texas in front of the capital to protest a bill that would deny voting access to poor Black and Brown communities. Afterward, we were invited into the office of more than one Texas representative to share about the issues hurting our community and to pray with and over them. Protesting in humble, nonviolent forms allows the church to have a credible witness to the watching world that we believe in the dignity of all peoples and that we are willing to suffer the cost of public protest, whatever that might be.

To express any or all of these forms of solidarity will require the local church to do things that put its own comfort and well-being at risk. Racial solidarity is messy. It always comes at a cost. But we must also recognize that there is no hope for cross-cultural relationships within the church if racial pains are never addressed. Dividing people into us-versus-them within the church is a problem as old as humanity itself. In every age and every country, the people of God have found ways to create divisions for who is worthy of attention and who is not. Church, if we want to have any hopes of pursuing racial solidarity as the body of Christ we must not lose sight of who our brothers and sisters are.

May we hold onto a robust understanding of the family of God, so that we can fully articulate and live into gospel-rooted solidarity. In the midst of much confusion and frustration surrounding the problems of race today, let us recapture a biblical theology of racial solidarity, so that we can cling to Scripture *and* make space for each other's stories and pains.

BIBLIOGRAPHY

Bradley, Anthony. "General Introduction: My Story." In *Aliens in the Promised Land: Why Minority Leadership Is Overlooked in White Christian Churches and Institutions*, edited by Anthony Bradley, 13–28. Phillipsburg, NJ: P&R, 2013.

Calvin, John. *The Epistles of Paul the Apostle to the Galatians, Ephesians, Philippians and Colossians*. Edited by David W. Torrance and Thomas F. Torrance. Calvin's Commentaries. Grand Rapids: Eerdmans, 1996.

Emerson, M. O., and D. H. Sikkink. "Portraits of American Life Study, 1st Wave, 2006." *Association of Religion Data Archives*, 4 Feb 2020. https://www.thearda.com/Archive/Files/Analysis/PALS/PALS_Var11_1.asp.

———. "Portraits of American Life Study, 2nd Wave, 2012." *Association of Religion Data Archives*, 25 Apr. 2020. https://www.thearda.com/Archive/Files/Analysis/PALS_2/PALS_2_Var708_1.asp.

Fobes, Clark. "The Privilege of Single-Issue Voting." *Fallen but Forgiven* (blog), 29 Oct 2020. https://clarkfobes.com/2020/10/29/the-privilege-of-single-issue-voting/.

Hays, J. Daniel. *From Every People and Nation: A Biblical Theology of Race*. Downers Grove, IL: InterVarsity, 2003.

Keener, Craig. *Galatians: A Commentary*. Grand Rapids: Baker Academic, 2019.

Matthews, Kenneth A., and M. Sydney Park. *The Post-Racial Church: A Biblical Framework for Multiethnic Reconciliation*. Grand Rapids: Kregel, 2011.

Redmond, Eric C. "Embracing the Other to the Glory of God." Plenary talk presented at a Center for Pastor Theologians conference, Oak Park, IL, 18 Oct 2021.

Reyes, Michelle Ami. *Becoming All Things: How Small Changes Lead to Lasting Connections across Cultures*. Grand Rapids: Zondervan, 2021.

Schreiner, Thomas R. *Galatians*. Exegetical Commentary on the New Testament. Grand Rapids: Zondervan, 2010.

"White Christians Have Become Even Less Motivated to Address Racial Injustice." *Barna*, 15 Sept 2020. https://www.barna.com/research/american-christians-race-problem/.

Williams, Jarvis J. *Redemptive Kingdom Diversity: A Biblical Theology of the People of God*. Grand Rapids: Baker Academic, 2021.

Wintle, Brian C., et al. *South Asia Bible Commentary: A One-Volume Commentary on the Whole Bible*. Grand Rapids: Zondervan Academic, 2015.

Yellow Horse, Aggie J., et al. "Stop AAPI Hate National Report: 3/19/20–6/30/21." *Stop AAPI Hate*. https://stopaapihate.org/stop-aapi-hate-national-report-2/.

7

Confronting Racial Injustice through Whole-Life Worship

Romans 12:1–2

RAYMOND CHANG

Therefore, I urge you, brothers and sisters, in view of God's mercy, to offer your bodies as a living sacrifice, holy and pleasing to God—this is your true and proper worship. Do not conform to the pattern of this world, but be transformed by the renewing of your mind. Then you will be able to test and approve what God's will is—his good, pleasing and perfect will.

ROM 12:1–2 NIV

THE CALL OF THE Christian is the call to worship. To worship is the primary purpose of the people of God. Christians are called to live our lives unto the glory of God. And as we see in 1 Cor 10:31, whether we eat or drink, and in all that we do, we are to do it unto God's glory. This is the call upon those who declare their allegiance to Christ.

But if I were to ask you to define worship, how would you define it? What does it mean to worship God?

In Romans 12, we find one of the most informative definitions of worship throughout Scripture. What we see here is so significant that N. T. Wright comments that "Paul's whole written work could be seen as an extended application of Romans 12:1–2."[1] In Rom 12:1, Paul writes: "Therefore, I urge you, brothers and sisters, in view of God's mercy, to offer your bodies as a living sacrifice, holy and pleasing to God—this is your true and proper worship."

After laying the theological framework for God's redeeming activity in the world from Romans 1–11, Paul pivots to the ethical implications of being recipients of God's superabundant mercy. After sharing about the ways God's mercies played out in human history, culminating in the person and work of Jesus Christ, Paul turns in chapter 12 from exposition to exhortation, from creed to conduct, from doctrine to duty, from belief to behavior, from the indicative to the imperative, and from orthodoxy to orthopraxy. But this shift isn't moving from theology to ethics as if they were two separate entities, but from one aspect of the gospel to another—more akin to looking at a sculpture from different angles.

And after he forges the theological framework, his first order of business is to call the people of God to worship God in consideration of all that God has done. This is what Paul means by saying "in view of God's mercy." In view of God's marvelous mercies, the first thing Paul calls for is to offer our bodies as a living sacrifice, holy and pleasing to God. This is how worship is defined here.

To worship God is to offer the entirety of one's being to him. God doesn't want just parts of us; he wants the whole of us. And in light of all that Christ has done, true and proper worship means that we offer all of ourselves to God. And as Romans is written to an entire church, it is a call to offer our whole selves to God in community.

So why am I bringing up this notion of worship when I am supposed to be talking about confronting racial injustice?

Simply put, I believe that racial injustice (especially the racial injustice that exists within and emerges from the church) is the byproduct of false and malformed worship. I don't think the problems of race and racism are primarily a sociological problem; instead, they are primarily a doxological problem.

The church is intended to be an outpost of God's kingdom. As such, it ought to reflect the kingdom of God to the world. In order to do so, it needs to possess the proper posture, practices, and priorities of worship, which is why Paul writes in verse 2, "Do not conform to the pattern of this world, but be transformed by the renewing of your mind."

But we cannot be transformed by the renewing of our mind if we remain conformed to the pattern of this world. In the words of James, "friendship

1. Wright, *Paul and the Faithfulness*, 1123.

with the world means enmity against God" (Jas 4:4 NIV). Said more seriously in the same verse, "anyone who chooses to be a friend of the world becomes an enemy of God." Conformity to the pattern of this world begins with a friendship with the world that puts us in opposition to God himself.

Conformity to the world hinders the transformation to which we are called. The two are at odds with one another. And whether we like it or not, our true and proper worship depends on this transformation. As Doug Moo writes, "The transformed life is not an optional second step after we embrace the gospel: it is rooted in, and indeed part of, the gospel itself."[2]

This is why we are called by God's word to be what Dr. Martin Luther King Jr. describes as "transformed nonconformists."[3] He goes on to say, "We are called to be people of conviction, not conformity; of moral nobility, not social respectability. We are commanded to live differently and according to a higher standard."[4]

Yet, when we look around, especially when it comes to issues of race, the evangelical church (and I speak as someone who longs to see the evangelical movement shift towards faithfulness on these issues) reflects the patterns of the world more than it reflects the kingdom of God. Far too often, the church falls in line with the patterns of racialization and racism more than it resists it. As a result, the church is as racialized, or even more racialized, than the surrounding world.

We know this in part by the fact that, on average, churches in the United States are still more segregated than the neighborhoods they are in. In fact, a study released in 2019 reveals that the average church in the United States is still four times more segregated than the neighborhood in which it resides.[5] This is especially tragic when you consider how housing in the United States still remains fairly segregated.

For the church to be more segregated than the already-segregated neighborhood it is in means that the church in the United States *participates* in racial segregation more than it is a force for *leading* in the work of racial healing and unity. We know this, because even when there is an emphasis on diversity, there is often an unwillingness to promote racial justice—which is simply making what is broken whole and righting the wrongs that have been committed. And diversity without justice—both in the world and in the church—leads to tokenism and perpetuates racial injustices that have real material impact. Sadly, instead of looking like outposts of God's kingdom, our

2. Moo, *Letter to the Romans*, 763.

3. King, *Strength to Love*, 11.

4. King, *Strength to Love*, 12.

5. Dougherty et al., "Racial Diversity."

communities and congregations reflect and propagate the patterns of racialization that consume the world.

Further, if churches happen to be racially diverse and not racially segregated, more often than not they maintain the same patterns of racial dominance and exclusion that we see in the world. Far too often the same racialized logic and attitudes we see in the world keep emerging within the church itself.

One of the persistent realities of the evangelical church is that the experiences of Christians of color often reveal that our churches reflect the world more than they reflect Christ. This failure to reflect kingdom priorities has led to a series of departures from predominantly white churches and denominations by Christians of color, especially by African Americans. We saw this with hip-hop artist Lecrae, who divorced himself from white Evangelicalism in 2017. And then with a series of prominent Black pastors, who departed from the Southern Baptist Convention in 2021. But they aren't the only ones. These departures confirm broader trends that were highlighted in the *The New York Times*, where the quiet exodus of Black Christians from evangelical churches was documented.[6] Christian sociologists like Michael Emerson also found that there has been a decrease in Black Christians who attend multiethnic churches (which are still primarily led by white pastors at 70 percent).[7] The percentage of African Americans attending multiracial churches declined from 27 percent to 21 percent in the seven years between 2012 and 2019, after a steady rise for years before that.[8] And who knows what those numbers looked like after 2020, which included the murder of George Floyd and culminated with the Capitol riots by many who held up Christian symbols in January of 2021? What people like Lecrae and the black pastors have done publicly, so many others have done quietly.

I can't tell you how many conversations I've had with racially minoritized Christians who have been devastated by their experiences in the white evangelical church. And this devastation has led to the shipwreck of so many people's faiths. I think two Black women summed it up best when they told me that they "expected the church to be a refuge from the world, but instead, found the world to very much be within the church." This was after trying for years to help their church improve in its racial efforts. This is perhaps why Dr. King proclaimed:

> Nowhere is the tragic tendency to conform more evident than in the church, an institution that has often served to crystallize,

6. Robertson, "Quiet Exodus."

7. Gjelten, "Multiracial Congregations."

8. Dougherty et al., "Racial Diversity."

conserve, and even bless the patterns of majority opinion. The erstwhile sanction by the church of slavery, racial segregation, war, and economic exploitation is testimony to the fact that the church has hearkened more to the authority of the world than to the authority of God. Called to be the moral guardian of the community, the church at times has preserved that which is immoral and unethical. Called to combat social evils, it has remained silent behind stained-glass windows. Called to lead men on the highway of brotherhood and to summon them to rise above the narrow confines of race and class, it has enunciated and practiced racial exclusiveness.[9]

Do not conform to the patterns of the world, but be transformed by the renewing of your mind.

To conform to the patterns of the world is to be, as King described, "like a thermometer, registering and reflecting the temperature all around us," when in fact we as Christians, "are called to be thermostats, influencing and changing the spiritual, moral, and cultural atmosphere of the society in which we live."[10] Unfortunately, as long as we allow the racializing forces of the world—which elevate and perpetuate the racialized visions and ways of being of the dominant racial group—to infiltrate and permeate the church, we will remain conformed to the patterns of the world more than we are transformed by the Spirit of God. And if we do, we will not be able to test and approve what God's will is—his good, pleasing, and perfect will.

So, then, what are we to do?

To be transformed by the renewing of our minds is to experience a transformation by God that reaches down to the deepest levels of who we are. As conformity to the world is no superficial matter, neither is transformation by the renewing of our minds. This transformation actively resists conformity to the world. It goes beyond impression management and the politics of respectability. It is a part of offering the whole of ourselves to God in worship. And this transformation occurs as the mind is renewed, as moral consciousness and practical reasoning are calibrated to the newness of our lives in the Spirit.

This is what the Scriptures identify as sanctification.

Sadly, when it comes to combating racism and racial injustice in the church, there are many who claim to be saved but refuse to be sanctified. They declare their salvation in Christ but reject sanctification in him. We know this because there is an active resistance to substantively and definitively addressing the forces of racialization and racism within the church.

9. King, *Strength to Love*, 15–16.
10. King, *Strength to Love*, 14.

We know we have conformed to the world when we actively oppose efforts to work against the powers and principalities that perpetuate all forms of racialization and racial injustice. This resistance comes in many forms, and all of them fall in line with the patterns of a racialized world.

One expression of this is the constant dismissal and denial of the lived experiences of the racially minoritized members of Christ's body. If not a dismissal and denial, there is frequent minimization. "That can't be true" and "They couldn't have meant it that way" and "It's not that bad" cycle over and over again.

Another way that the evangelical church has resisted meaningful efforts to confront racism and racial injustice is that for too long, Evangelicals— namely, white Evangelicals—have been overwhelmingly negligent (if not outright resistant) about developing theology around race. Those who have offered a convicting perspective on the issue have been often viewed with suspicion and therefore overlooked, disregarded, or even disparaged. This occurs as many have little to no trouble embracing and justifying the works of theologians and pastors who advocated for slavery, promoted Jim Crow segregation, supported Chinese exclusion, turned a blind eye to Japanese incarceration camps, and completely ignored the reality that we continue to reap the benefits of stolen land. These same theologians and pastors had their fair share of damning indiscretions that many ignore, and yet it is remarkable how frequently Dr. King's sins are brought up while the sins of others seem to go unnoticed.

As a result of this, the unbelieving world has done what the evangelical movement has failed to do by producing research and thinking that is often far more robust and far more consistent with the weight of reality. Where the church tapped out, the unbelieving world tapped in through the common grace of God to help name what is so plain among those who are racially minoritized.

Sadly, instead of contending with the work like some are doing, many Evangelicals struggle to use the words that best describe the thing being addressed. This, in part, is leading the evangelical movement to display the same problems around race that we see in the world. The church offers very little that is considered compelling when it comes to the ways that faith impacts the racialized realities in which we find ourselves. We have become adept at telling people what they should not do, but we have failed to adequately produce a theology that shows the world—and the church—what a full and meaningful life in community and our public Christian witness can look like to a racialized society.

There are many other ways we have conformed to the world, but I want to focus on one of the other prominent patterns that has been adopted by the evangelical world, and that is through a war on words.

One of the tactics that the world has consistently employed is to soften the language used when describing racial injustice and oppression in order to preserve the racial status quo.

For instance, if you look at the Japanese incarceration, those in power adamantly called it "internment." People would soften the language of racial injustice by using terms like "evacuee" or "internee" instead of "inmate," "detainee," and "prisoner"; "evacuation" instead of "forced removal"; and "relocation center'" instead of "illegal detention center." The words were intentionally utilized to minimize the unconstitutional atrocities committed to 120,000 people of Japanese ancestry (two-thirds of whom were American). As George Orwell writes, "If thought corrupts language, language can also corrupt thought."[11] The American evangelical world has adopted this pattern of diluting language to call racism something less than what it is, and as a result, the diluted language has corrupted much thought.

Following the patterns of the world, as language around injustice and evil is diluted, thought is corrupted; and as thought is corrupted, far too many of us conform to the patterns of the world. As a result, our ability to test and approve what God's will is—his good, pleasing, and perfect will—is compromised. What we see is that you can't heal what you won't diagnose. You can't fix what you can't name.

Think of words like "privilege," "racism," and "white supremacy" and how we are often hindered from and even penalized for using the terms that most accurately describe a reality. I still remember being told to use the word "advantage" instead of "privilege," "prejudice" or "bias" instead of "racism," and to avoid using the term "white supremacy" at all if I wanted to keep being invited to speak. And I have found that in the evangelical world, the less you talk about white supremacy, the more you tend to be embraced. It's worth asking why, when we have seen it consistently played out through history, through law, through education policies, through housing policies, through citizenship, and more.

But what I have also found is that the less we use the words, the more we spend our time trying to figure out what we actually need to talk about. And the less we use the words, the less we actually understand what these realities really are. There is power in naming, which is why racism doesn't want to be named.

11. Orwell, *Politics and English Language*, page unknown.

I do want to clarify that language is and always has been tricky. It will take time to cultivate understanding, which is exactly what we are called to do as pastors, preachers, teachers, and theologians. This means that we ourselves must commit to unlearning the patterns of the world and learning the ways of God. We must commit to the deep work of understanding how race and racism function and operate in both the church and the broader society. And as we commit to transformation through the renewal of our minds, we also commit to walking with others in the renewal of theirs. In our work towards confronting racial injustice so that we might live into the unity that Christ established, and in our commitment to displaying the fullness of the gospel, we might have to start with where people are; but as God never abandoned us in our ignorance, we should not abandon others.

With that said, when it comes to combating racial injustice, we have to understand that the social construction of race is rooted in the preservation, the promotion, and the propagation of white supremacy. The entire racial construct was built around the idea that whiteness in all of its ways is superior to everything else. In fact, blackness was created as a contrast to whiteness, and categories like Asian American and Latin@ emerged as a way to be seen in the midst of erasure. Even the terms "Native American" or "Indian" erased important tribal distinctions. Ta-Nahesi Coates writes that "race is the child of racism."[12] And race, at its core, was created to build up, prop up, and privilege those who were categorized as white. This means that we cannot meaningfully talk about or address issues of race, racialization, and racism without talking about whiteness and white supremacy.

It's important to note, when race scholars talk about whiteness and white supremacy, they are not talking about all "white" people—or all people who have a phenotype or physical features that are associated with what is often understood to be white. To assume that whiteness is primarily a biological notion of race is a fundamental flaw in thinking when it comes to race, which actually reveals that people don't know what race is and how it functions. Whiteness is an ideology with profound material effects that forces people to choose between assimilation and annihilation.

I know that people don't understand what race is when they can't use the term white. And as I just mentioned, anyone who understands race, knows that whiteness does not mean all white people. And I would like to suggest that if we can't talk about whiteness and white supremacy, we really can't talk about race in any meaningful manner. And a failure to talk about race in any meaningful manner is rampant in the evangelical church. When people use euphemistic terms like Caucasian, you know they are living under the thumb

12. Coates, *Between the World and Me*, 7.

of white supremacy. You know that their understanding of whiteness is thin, because to be Caucasian means you can trace your genealogy back to the Caucasus region (which makes me feel bad for Italians, Germans, Norwegians, etc.). But notice how often people will avoid using the word white, even when they don't have trouble using the term Black or African American, Asian American, or Latino, which are also racial categories—just like white is.

I was speaking at a Christian conference several years ago, and a fellow speaker was going back and forth about whether she should use the phrase white supremacy or white superiority. She told me that she was going to use the word superiority because she was afraid that saying white supremacy would simply shut people down. When I saw her a few years later, she said that decision really weighed on her, because she felt like she had compromised in fear. She said she knew that she was catering to white supremacy by not naming it in order to gain approval, which is consistent with what Willie Jennings says about whiteness—that it likes to hide in plain sight. This does not mean she didn't take the time to explain it, but that she explained it and still didn't name white supremacy for what it was. And though she gained the approval of the dominant white majority by softening the language, it came as a discouragement to the racialized minorities who needed someone to be straightforward in their rebuke of it. Like calling sin a mistake or Satan a negative, both to her and to many others, it felt diluted.

Words matter, especially when they are able to name things as they are. Words are powerful, especially when they can identify the strongholds that are hindering us. Words are liberating, especially when they stand against evil and promote good. And words can lead to worship, especially as they are grounded in the truth of God and in the truth of reality.

Words find their meaning in context—in the sacred interactions between people who bear the image of God. When we resist the urge to argue over words, we can begin to really do the deep work of seeing and understanding each other. It's only then that we will be transformed and, in so doing, worship!

As Christians, we have the great privilege of being able to offer our lives to the living God as an act of worship. This is the great privilege that allows us to sacrifice every other privilege we might possess. But we cannot enter into true and proper worship as long as we maintain and perpetuate the patterns of racism. To offer the entirety of ourselves as a living sacrifice is to work against the powers and principalities of racialization and racism. It cannot be done by pretending like it doesn't exist, minimizing its effects, or refusing to name the evil that it is. And make no mistake, racism is evil. The only way it can be done is by telling the truth about it.

I don't expect much from the world, but I hope for much from the church. And as such, my prayer is that Christians will offer alternative visions to the racialized world in which we live as we truly become cities on hills and lights to the world that display a vision of God's kingdom.

BIBLIOGRAPHY

Coates, Ta-Nehisi. *Between the World and Me*. Melbourne: Text, 2020.

Dougherty, Kevin D., et al. "Racial Diversity in U.S. Congregations, 1998–2019." *Journal for the Scientific Study of Religion* 59.4 (Dec 2020) 651–62. https://doi.org/10.1111/jssr.12681.

Gjelten, Tom. "Multiracial Congregations May Not Bridge Racial Divide." *NPR*, 17 July 2020. https://www.npr.org/2020/07/17/891600067/multiracial-congregations-may-not-bridge-racial-divide.

King, Martin Luther, Jr. *Strength to Love*. Boston: Beacon, 2019.

Moo, Douglas J. *The Letter to the Romans*. NICNT. Grand Rapids: Eerdmans, 1974.

Orwell, George. *Politics and the English Language*. London: Renard, 2021.

Robertson, Campbell. "A Quiet Exodus: Why Black Worshipers Are Leaving White Evangelical Churches." *The New York Times*, 9 Mar 2018. https://www.nytimes.com/2018/03/09/us/blacks-evangelical-churches.html.

Wright, N. T. *Paul and the Faithfulness of God*. Minneapolis: Fortress, 2013.

8

Racism and Original Sin

Insights from the Christian East

GERALD HIESTAND

JIM WALLIS, IN HIS book *America's Original Sin: Racism, White Privilege, and the Bridge to a New America*, frequently refers (as the title portends) to racism as America's "original sin."[1] Wallis's assertion is clearly connected to Christianity's long-standing doctrine of the same name, which speaks to humanity's collective guilt and corruption that resulted from Adam's primordial sin in Eden. In the same way that the sin of Adam, the founding father of humanity, implicated all of his posterity in corruption and guilt, so too, Wallis argues, the exploitation of indigenous and African people by America's founding fathers has implicated all of their (white) posterity in corruption and guilt.

For Wallis, the analogical comparison of original sin to racism is apt insofar as the effect of America's racism has not been limited to a single generation.[2] Just as Adam's sin continues to linger in his descendants, the residue of America's racist founding has lingered in the lives of Americans. Wallis highlights the disparities within the criminal justice system, the clear anti-black

---

1. Wallis, *America's Original Sin*. Wallis's connection between racism and original sin dates as far back as his essay "America's Original Sin," in *Sojourners* (1987).

2. It is worth noting that Wallis (from what I can tell) is using original sin as a *theological analogy*. He is not claiming that racism has been passed from George Washington to George Bush (for example) in the exact same way, with the same metaphysical mechanisms by which Adam's sin was passed on to his posterity.

bias of too many police officers, and the economic and educational inequity of contemporary society as evidence that America's racist past continues to linger on as an oppressive evil power.[3]

Wallis acknowledges that the connection between racism and original sin is provocative. But he thinks the connection is both helpful and needed:

> The language of "America's original sin" helped me understand that the historical racism against America's Indigenous people and enslaved Africans was indeed a *sin*, and one upon which this country was founded . . . if we are able to recognize that the sin still lingers, we can better understand issues before us today and deal with them more deeply, honestly, and even spiritually—which is essential if we are to make real progress toward solutions.[4]

The reception of Wallis's association between racism and original sin has been mixed. On the whole, theological liberals have resonated with the association, while theological conservatives have not.[5] There is a certain irony here. Those on the theological left don't generally go in for the doctrine of original sin, most especially the Western Augustinian version. Why, then, are they so quick to apply it to the sin of racism? And those on the theological right are generally quite supportive of the doctrine of original sin. Why, then, are theological conservatives so quick to dismiss it with the sin of racism?

The issues at work here are complex—not only theologically but also sociologically and culturally. And of course, we human beings are not always consistent in our theological reasoning. But I suspect that the liberal inclination to connect racism and original sin and the conservative impulse to reject the connection are related to the fact that both sides are (consciously or subconsciously) working from a Western Augustinian notion of original sin that entails both inherited corruption *and* inherited guilt.[6] It is, I will suggest, the Western concept of inherited guilt that creates much of the difficulty when

3. Wallis, *America's Original Sin*, xxvi.

4. Wallis, *America's Original Sin*, xxiv; italics in original. The word *lingering* shows up frequently in Wallis's book, especially in his introduction. Just like Adamic sin continues to impact Adam's posterity, so too America's original sin has a similar lingering power that negatively impacts white Americans.

5. See, for instance, Kevin DeYoung's "Reparations: A Critical Theological Review." DeYoung does not interact with Wallis's book but more generally critiques the connection between racism and original sin.

6. From what I can tell, Wallis is not intentionally choosing between the Western and Eastern approaches to original sin. Insofar as the Western articulation of original sin is dominant in America, the Western framework serves as the assumed framework in Wallis's use of the doctrine.

drawing a connection between racism and original sin. In my view, the Western conception of original sin as a metaphor for race is a theological overreach that undermines, rather than serves, race conversations in America.

But the Western notion of original sin is not Christianity's only articulation of the doctrine. The other half of the church, as embodied by the Eastern Orthodox tradition, offers Christianity another account of original sin that affirms the reality of inherited corruption but, unlike the West, denies inherited guilt.[7] This Eastern Orthodox account of original sin is, I believe, more useful for race conversations.

Toward that end, the aim of this paper is to clarify Christianity's Eastern Orthodox understanding of original sin vis-à-vis its Western counterpart and suggest that the logic of the Eastern Orthodox position is more readily useful (and applicable) for helping theologically minded Americans make sense of the lingering power of racism in America.

Before proceeding, however, it is worth noting two things. First, this paper is written in conscious support of folks like Wallis who recognize that America's racist origins continue to have an ongoing effect in American culture. As such, this paper assumes rather than defends the premise that informal racist structures, patterns of learned behavior, and systems continue to exist in American culture. Like Wallis, I agree that these informal structures are the residue of America's explicit and formal institution of slavery and our treatment of indigenous people.

Second, my intent in this essay is not to argue in favor of the Eastern Orthodox position on original sin over and against the Western articulation (I remain sympathetic to the Western articulation). Rather, my aim is more narrowly to suggest that the interior logic of the Eastern Orthodox position is more *useful* for explaining and elucidating America's racist history. Thus, my concern is primarily pragmatic.

Enough throat clearing. The essay is divided into three main parts. The first part will detail the Western notion of original sin as both inherited corruption and inherited guilt. The second part will detail the Eastern Orthodox articulation of original sin as limited to inherited corruption. And the final

7. For those unfamiliar with the East and West distinction in Christian history, it will be helpful to know that Western (Latin) Christianity traces its roots back to Rome, the western capital of the Roman Empire, and the Roman Catholic Church, to include the Protestant churches that broke away from Roman Catholicism in the sixteenth century. Eastern (Greek) Christianity traces its roots back to Constantinople, the eastern capital of the Roman Empire, and the Eastern Orthodox church, to include the various national and semiautonomous churches that make up Eastern Orthodoxy (e.g., Russian Orthodox, Greek Orthodox, etc.) The Eastern and Western traditions developed together in basic theological unity for the first thousand years of Christian history but formally separated in the eleventh century over matters of Christology.

part of the essay will offer a few suggestions about how the Eastern doctrine of original sin can be helpfully used in contemporary race conversations.

We begin with the Western Augustinian articulation of original sin.

I. Original Sin in the Western Augustinian Tradition

Saint Augustine, the fifth-century North African bishop of Hippo, is justifiably praised (or blamed) for the West's understanding of original sin. The idea of original sin can be found in both the Old and New Testaments and was known in less precise ways in the early church prior to Augustine. But it is Augustine's robust articulation of the doctrine—seen especially against the backdrop of his controversy with Pelagius, the British heretic-monk—that shaped Western conceptions of the doctrine in both the Roman Catholic tradition and the "magisterial" Protestant traditions that broke with Rome in the sixteenth century. (Luther and Calvin, the two most significant Protestant Reformers, followed the basic Augustinian articulation.) Two important elements of Augustine's doctrine are especially noteworthy for our purposes—his idea of inherited *corruption* and his notion of inherited *guilt*.

A. Original Sin and Inherited Corruption

Augustine introduces Adam at the top of the created hierarchy. Adam is complete and mature at the moment of creation, a spiritual and physical adult possessing all the moral resources needed for living in faithful obedience to God.[8] In the words of Augustine, Adam is *posse peccare et posse non peccare*—able to sin and able not to sin—fully free to follow God's law. But the felicity of Adam was short lived. He misused his freedom and disobeyed God's command. The results were disastrous. Adam's first act of sin severed his relationship with God and rendered him incapable of living a righteous life. Immediately he became *non posse non peccare*—not able not to sin.[9]

Narrowly speaking, Augustine uses the expression "original sin" to denote the first sinful *act* of Adam, whereby he transgressed the divine law of Eden and ate the forbidden fruit. But more often, Augustine uses the expression to refer to the resulting ontological *corruption* that stemmed from Adam's first sinful act. Insofar as Adam's life was bound up in God's life, his severing from God resulted in the corruption and disintegration of Adam's life.

---

8. Augustine, *Literal Meaning of Genesis*, 6.18.

9. Augustine, *Rebuke and Grace*, in NPNF1, 33.

95

The effects of Adam's sin reached deep into the spiritual core of Adam's very being; he became ruined from the inside out. For Augustine, Adam's disobedience resulted in spiritual "disease," a disordering of his affections after the fashion of brute "beasts," and a loss of control over the body.[10] By willingly choosing to transgress the law of God, Adam plunged himself into spiritual and moral ruin from which he was unable to return. Divine punishment for Adam's sin followed closely—physical death, to match Adam's self-inflicted spiritual death.

But Adam's fall into sin and death was not for him alone. Adam, who contained within himself all of humanity, corrupted not only himself but all subsequent humanity with him. Here, Augustine's ontological realism is an important concept for his understanding of original sin.[11] For Augustine, the whole of human nature was a single substance really and truly present within Adam when he sinned. As such, the entirety of human nature was tainted by Adam's sin the moment he fell.[12] Individual men and women born from Adam's line necessarily contained within themselves this tainted human nature and were themselves necessarily born with Adam's corruption. Like a stream that flows out of a polluted lake, Adam's posterity is downstream from Adam and thus inherently and inevitably polluted by Adam's corruption. Thus, Augustine can write that "[Adam], in whom all die . . . depraved also in his own person all who come from his stock by the hidden corruption of his own carnal concupiscence."[13] He goes on to call original sin a "fatal flaw," which has "so far prevailed, that all men are born with the fault of original sin."[14] Augustine scholar Eugene Portalie helpfully captures some of Augustine's more vivid language regarding the effect of Adam's sin upon his posterity. For Augustine, Adam's line is "a mass of slime; a mass of sin, of sins, of iniquity; a mass of wrath, of death, of damnation, of offense; a mass totally vitiated, damnable, damned."[15]

Augustine's debate with the British monk Pelagius helped clarify (and solidify) his position on the corruption and transmission of original sin. Pelagius found Augustine's doctrine of original sin far too anthropologically

10. Augustine, *On the Merits and Remission of Sins, and on the Baptism of Infants*, in NPNF1, 1.21.

11. For a helpful discussion of Augustine's realism, see Portalie, *Guide to the Thought*, 204–13; see also McGiffert, *History of Christian Thought*, 91–92.

12. Augustine is working from the same realist perspective that the author of Hebrews uses when he suggests that Levi paid tithes to Melchizedek while yet in the loins of Abraham (Heb 7:4–10).

13. Augustine, *On the Merits*, in NPNF1, 1.10.

14. Augustine, *On Original Sin*, in NPNF1, 2.46.

15. Portalie, *Guide to the Thought*, 212.

pessimistic. Human beings, Pelagius insisted, are not helpless captives of Adam's sin. The ability to obey the divine commands must be within reach, lest God's commands be senseless. For Pelagius and his allies, sin was not a substance but an act. It was not a "thing" that could corrupt a person's nature; therefore, sin could not be passed from parent to child. As moving the arm does not change the arm, Pelagius argued, so too the exercise of the will in a sinful act does not change the intrinsic nature of a person nor render him or his offspring incapable of fulfilling God's law.[16]

This was all good news for Adam's posterity. Since sin did not corrupt the sinner's ontology, the offspring of Adam did not enter the world spiritually corrupted by sin. For Pelagius, each human being entered the world in the same condition as Adam on the day of his creation—innocent and fully *posse non peccare*, fully able not to sin. Adam's original sin was for Adam alone.

Pelagius's conception of sin as an act rather than a substance was clever (heretics are nothing if not clever). It was all the more clever because the idea of evil as a nonsubstance was Augustine's own. Augustine, along with the other theologically orthodox church fathers, commonly referred to sin and evil as a privation, a "nonthing" that had no ontological substance.[17] How could a nonthing be passed from parent to child, Pelagius wanted to know?

But Augustine was undeterred. He countered Pelagius's logic by using the analogy of eating.[18] Eating (or not eating) was an act and not a substance; yet, eating was an act that changed the substance of the body. In the same way, the act of sinning, though itself an act and not a substance, nonetheless changed the substance of the soul. Though original sin was not technically a substance, the effects of it were truly substantive. Adam's one act of original sin resulted in a universal condition of moral depravity that could indeed be passed to his descendants.

B. Original Sin as Inherited Guilt

But for Augustine, the situation was more dire still. Not only did he insist on inherited corruption, he likewise insisted on inherited guilt. Here again,

16. Augustine, *On Nature and Grace*, in NPNF1, 1.21.

17. So too did the majority of Christians in Augustine's day. Augustine (and the other church fathers) viewed sin as a privation, a nonthing. As cold is to heat and darkness is to light, so sin is the absence of good rather than the presence of some tangible quality of evil. Augustine contends that it is permissible to speak of sin as a substance in the same way that we often speak of cold or darkness as a substance, while understanding them in a technical sense to be a privation of a substance (see TeSelle, *Augustine the Theologian*, 144).

18. Augustine, *On Nature and Grace*, in NPNF1, 1.22.

Augustine's realism comes into play. For Augustine, since Adam and his descendants were all "one man," the sin of Adam was truly and really the sin of his descendants. Augustine distinguishes between two types of sin: the personal sin that each person commits that is particular to himself alone and the one common sin that every person committed along with Adam when Adam first sinned. He writes,

> It is surely clear enough that the sins which are peculiar to every man, which they themselves commit and which belong simply to them mean one thing; and that the one sin [i.e., original sin], in and by which all have sinned, means another thing: *since all were that one man.*[19]

In other words, since all of humanity was truly present in Adam when Adam sinned, all of humanity justly bears responsibility for Adam's transgression. Here, Augustine has more than legal imputation in mind.[20] His idea is not that God holds each person accountable for a sin that they themselves did not really commit. Rather, each person *really did* commit Adam's sin *in Adam* and thus are justly held guilty for Adam's sin. Though they have no memory of it, Adam's posterity really did commit sin in Adam.

In his book *On the Soul and Its Origin*, Augustine lists four precautions to consider when discussing the origin of the soul. His second precaution is that one must not teach that "the soul becomes sinful by another's original sin."[21] For Augustine, the descendants of Adam are bound up in Adam's sin not simply by divine fiat but because Adam's descendants were truly present in Adam when he sinned; they were one with Adam, indeed, they were "all that one man." Thus, the sin of Adam was, and truly is, the sin of his descendants. "Because they were clothed with the flesh of him who sinned in his will, they contract from him the responsibility for sin."[22]

But lest we worry that Augustine taught that we are damned solely on the basis of Adam's sin, he assures us that we all sin damnably too—on top of Adam's sin. For Augustine, Adam's guilt was sufficient to damn his posterity, but the guilt of original sin wasn't the only guilt in town. Humanity's inherited

---

19. Augustine, *On Forgiveness of Sins, and Baptism*, in NPNF1, 1.11 (italics added).

20. A number of Reformation theologians linked inherited guilt to imputation, using the same logic as their doctrine of justification. Just as Christ's righteousness is imputed to his posterity, so too Adam's sin is imputed to his posterity. And just as Christ's posterity did not truly fulfill the law, so too Adam's posterity did not truly sin Adam's sin.

21. Augustine, *On the Soul and Its Origin*, in NPNF1, 1.34.

22. *Incomplete Work against Julian*, §6 (as quoted in Portalie, *Guide to the Thought*, 211, from Migne's *Patrologiae latinae* 42, cols. 504–72). See also Augustine, *On Original Sin*, in NPNF1, 43.

corruption from Adam was the cause of personal sin and guilt for Adam's posterity. Each person born into Adam's sin inevitably followed in Adam's sinful footsteps. If Adam couldn't keep from sinning at the height of his perfection, how much less could those born into Adam's corruption? Thus, for Augustine, the common original sin of Adam is the explanation for why there is so much personal sin in Adam's posterity—sins of violence, injustice, hate, vice, and fleshly indulgence. (And racism.)

The Pelagian assault on Augustine's doctrine of original sin eventually necessitated a broader church response. Councils were called, bishops were gathered, and Augustine's doctrine of original sin was vindicated.[23] Pelagius, in denying the reality of original sin, had denied the need for grace.

II. ORIGINAL SIN IN THE CHRISTIAN EAST

But the triumph of Augustine over Pelagius was largely a Western triumph. The Christian East wasn't so sure. In the first centuries of the Christian East, the doctrine of original sin had moved in a somewhat kinder and less totalizing direction. Like Augustine and the West, the East generally worked within an ontological realist framework; and also like the West, the Eastern theologians tended to agree that all of humanity shared in Adam's *corruption*. But the language of the Eastern theologians was, on the whole, more sympathetic to the post-fall human condition. While they agreed that the ravages of Adam's sin had left no part of humanity untouched, Augustine's expression "mass of slime" was not an expression the Eastern theologians were wont to use. There was no one single theologian that shaped the East's notion of original sin (such as Augustine did in the West). But a number of theologians were particularly influential. In what follows, I highlight three Eastern theologians who each articulate an important aspect of the Eastern doctrine of original sin that relates to the connection between racism and original sin—Saint Irenaeus (second century), Saint Athanasius (fourth century), and Saint Cyril (fifth century).

23. In AD 418, a small nonecumenical council was assembled at Carthage, and Augustine's teaching on original sin was upheld over and against the Pelagian critique. A later, larger ecumenical council was gathered in Ephesus (431), and again the church ratified Augustine's position. A third council, the Second Council of Orange, was called in 529, and once more Augustine's basic position on original sin was upheld.

A. Saint Irenaeus and the Devil's Tyranny: The Greater the Sin, the Greater the Responsibility

Saint Irenaeus is the earliest extant theologian (East or West) to provide a robust account of Adam's fall and its impact on Adam's posterity.[24] In contrast to Augustine (and the West more generally), Irenaeus introduces us to Adam as a child-king who is destined to one day rule over the whole world. But that day is not the first day of creation. Since Adam is not created at the height of his maturity but rather in infancy, it was necessary that he grow over time into maturity prior to assuming the world's throne.[25]

In the meantime, one of the high archangels was appointed as a "steward"—along with the angels under him—to temporarily manage the affairs of the world until Adam came of age. Here's where Irenaeus's account of original sin begins. The steward was not content with his subservient status. Envious of Adam's royal privilege, the steward-angel desired the world's throne for himself. Why should a mighty archangel at the height of his powers release his sovereignty to one lesser than himself? He refused. Like Tolkien's Lord Denethor, the angelic steward of Eden would not relinquish his governance to the rightful king. And so the steward-angel became the devil.[26]

24. Irenaeus's comments on Adam's sin and its effect are found in his two extant works, *Demonstration of the Apostolic Preaching* and *Against Heresies*. All citations for Irenaeus are taken from MacKenzie, *Irenaeus's Demonstration*, and Coxe, *Apostolic Fathers*, respectively. It would be claiming too much to state that Irenaeus had a fully formed doctrine of original sin; he did not. But he did have a clear sense that Adam's sin negatively impacted Adam's posterity. As such, the basic building blocks of the doctrine are present in Irenaeus, even if the language is not.

25. Irenaeus, *Demonstration*, in MacKenzie, *Irenaeus's Demonstration*, 12, 14. See also Irenaeus, *Against Heresies*, in Coxe, *Apostolic Fathers*, 3.22.4, 3.23.5, 4.38.1–2. Whether literal or spiritual children is a matter of debate among Irenaeus scholars. My own reading of Irenaeus is that he conceives of Adam and Eve as literal prepubescent children. The idea of Adam and Eve as literal children is not the dominant idea in Eastern Orthodoxy, though it does appear in Theophilus and Clement. However, the Eastern Orthodox tradition does follow in Irenaeus's line of thought that Adam is not created in full maturity but must undergo spiritual development and growth before reaching his full perfection. See Steenberg, "Children in Paradise."

26. See Irenaeus, *Demonstration*, in MacKenzie, *Irenaeus's Demonstration*, 11–12. For Irenaeus, the devil's first sin was his envy of Adam's lordship over the earth. As such, the Eden temptation was the first occasion in which the steward-angel became the devil. This is in contrast to the Western account of the devil, in which the devil's first sin was pride against God in heaven and the devil's rebellion was directed against God/Christ's lordship of heaven. The Irenaean account continues to live on in the liturgical theology of Eastern Orthodoxy, even though some Eastern Orthodox theologians do not seem to recognize the difference between the Eastern and Western accounts. The Western account of the devil, such as we read in John Milton's *Paradise Lost*, began with Origen (also an Eastern theologian) but was given pride of place in the West through Augustine. For an

The temptation at the tree, then, was the outworking of the devil's plot to kill humanity and abscond with the world's throne. The steward-angel knew that God would not tolerate open rebellion against Adam's lordship. And so in subterfuge, he cloaked himself in the guise of the serpent and deceived Adam and Eve into sinning. Adam and Eve, still being children, were no match for the devil's cunning. They transgressed God's law and brought death upon themselves. Cut off from the sustaining life of God, humanity became corrupt, and spiritual death immediately took hold.[27]

But in gentleness and leniency, God did not curse Adam and Eve. They were but children, and the primary responsibility for their fall lay with the steward-angel. As such, God's curse passed to humanity only indirectly—consisting of toil in the ground and pain in childbearing.[28] But the full curse of God fell directly upon the devil: a Son of Eve would arise, who would overthrow the devil and cast him and his angels into the fires of hell.[29] Once the devil was vanquished, the promised Son of Eve would return humanity to the earth's royal throne.[30]

The consequences for Adam and Eve extended beyond God's indirect curse. God punished Adam and Eve with physical death for their disobedience, just as he said he would. He expelled them from Eden, and they lost access to the tree of life. This divine "death sentence" impacted all of Adam and Eve's posterity. Since the day of Adam's exile from Eden, all of humanity has likewise been sentenced to death, "tied up and bound with death through [Adam's] disobedience." Adam, in his sin, had "stricken down" all of humanity within himself.[31] Death and corruption took hold of humanity. But even in this judgment, the mercy of God for humanity still shone through. Had a corrupted humanity been allowed to remain in the garden with access to the tree of life, it would have eaten the tree's immortal fruit and lived forever in that corrupted state. In God's kindness and wisdom, physical death became a backward blessing, a divine remedy for death itself. God would use the physical death of Jesus—the true and Second Adam, the promised Son of Eve—as

---

executive summary of Irenaeus's account of the devil's fall, see Hiestand, "Irenaeus, the Devil."

27. Irenaeus, *Against Heresies*, in Coxe, *Apostolic Fathers*, 3.23.7; Irenaeus, *Demonstration*, in MacKenzie, *Irenaeus's Demonstration*, 31.

28. Irenaeus, *Against Heresies*, in Coxe, *Apostolic Fathers*, 3.23.3.

29. Irenaeus, *Against Heresies*, in Coxe, *Apostolic Fathers*, 3.23.5.

30. Notably, for Irenaeus (and Jesus!), the fires of hell were not originally created for rebellious humans but for rebellious angels. Human beings end up there only insofar as they side with the devil. See Irenaeus, *Against Heresies*, in Coxe, *Apostolic Fathers*, 4.40.1, 4.44.1, and Matt 25:41.

31. Irenaeus, *Demonstration*, in MacKenzie, *Irenaeus's Demonstration*, 31.

a means of freeing humanity from the corrupted body of death that humanity had come to inhabit.[32]

In the meantime, though, the earth's royal throne had been lost to the tyranny of the devil. Irenaeus likens the plight of Adam's posterity to a city that has been captured and enslaved by a tyrant. In the same way the descendants of a captured city are born into the slavery of their parents, so too all of humanity are born into a world enslaved by the devil and held under the power of sin and death.[33] This framing of Adam's original sin then shapes Irenaeus's well-known *Christus Victor* account of redemption. For Irenaeus, Christ is the Stronger Man who comes to rescue humanity from the unjust power of the devil. Jesus overthrows the tyrant, breaks his power of death, and brings to completion humanity's original royal destiny.[34]

Two elements of Irenaeus's narrative are worth noting. First, Irenaeus's emphasis on Adam's creation as a child, as well as the devil's ongoing tyranny, makes humanity as much a victim of sin as a perpetrator of sin. God does not judge Adam's sin and the devil's sin as moral equivalents. The devil is the first and greatest sinner. He, at the height of his powers, took advantage of Adam and Eve in their infancy. And with the devil's greater power came a greater culpability. As such, the devil receives the stiffer punishment. A way back to Eden is made for Adam and Eve; but there is no way back for the steward-angel.

Second, it's worth noting that the concept of inherited guilt does not factor into Irenaeus's account of Adam's sin. For Irenaeus, deliverance from the devil's tyranny and the Adamic corruption and death are the primary obstacles that Christ's redeeming work must overcome. The sin of an individual can significantly harm another, to be sure—even plunge another into corruption and death and enslavement to a tyrant. But each person, including Adam, is guilty only for his or her own sins. Thus, the plight of Adam's posterity is inherited corruption and enslavement to the devil's tyranny, not inherited guilt.

B. Saint Athanasius and Humanity's Share in Adamic Corruption

Saint Athanasius, like Irenaeus, articulates a notion of original sin that focuses on humanity's inherited plight, but with a particularly strong emphasis on humanity's share in Adam's ontological corruption. Athanasius's famous treatise *On the Incarnation* provides the main lines of his articulation of Adam's sin. In his treatise, Athanasius introduces human beings as a midway point between

---

32. Irenaeus, *Against Heresies*, in Coxe, *Apostolic Fathers*, 3.23.6–7.

33. Irenaeus, *Against Heresies*, in Coxe, *Apostolic Fathers*, 5.1.1.

34. Irenaeus, *Against Heresies*, in Coxe, *Apostolic Fathers*, 4.33.4.

God in heaven and the beasts on earth. God is immortal, immutable, and eternal. The beasts (like the rest of creation) are mortal, mutable, and finite; they were brought forth from nothing and are naturally prone to return to nothing. Human beings, while having an inherent "ontological poverty"[35] like all mere creatures, are nonetheless given a share in God's immortality through participation in the *imago Dei*.[36] The *imago Dei* is a gift beyond the lot of the other mortal creatures meant to point Adam to the true and eternal *imago Dei*—Jesus Christ, the one true human being.[37] As long as Adam lives in contemplation of the Word of God as his sole source of life, he will be kept from his inherent "natural" proclivity toward mutability and decay. But alas, Adam reaches above his station. In taking hold of the forbidden fruit, he strives to be noncontingent. Ironically and tragically, the only creature uniquely made to be like God strove to be his own god.

The gavel of divine judgment fell. God had promised that death would be the judicial punishment for disobedience, and indeed, God was true to his word. Humanity, in choosing to turn away from the contemplation of the divine, was punitively "released" to that which was "theirs by nature."[38] God would no longer stand in the way of humanity's ontological proclivity toward corruption and nonbeing. As a result of Adam's sin, death "gained from that time forth a legal hold over [humanity], and it was impossible to evade the law, since it had been laid down by God because of the transgression."[39]

Though Athanasius uses judicial language, such as legal hold and law, his soteriological frame is not focused on guilt, such as we find in Augustine. For Athanasius, the punishment of Adam and Eve was death. Inevitably, spiritually dead parents give birth to spiritually dead children. Like a receding wave of energy, all of humanity have since been born into Adam and Eve's dying life.[40] And in this sense, Adam's posterity cannot evade the judicial death sentence that has been passed on from Adam. The logic here is similar to Irenaeus's analogy of an enslaved city. The children born into an enslaved city are enslaved not because *they* lost the war to the tyrant, but because their parents did. Thus, the responsibility for the city's enslavement does not originate with the children but with parents. And yet, the children are caught up in the plight of the city all the same. In the same way, Adam and Eve's descendants are not guilty for the sin of their parents; Adam's sin was Adam's sin

35. I'm indebted to Khaled Anatolios for this apt expression. See his *Athanasius*, 58.

36. Athanasius, *Incarnation*, in Hardy, *Christology of the Later Fathers*, 7 .

37. Athanasius, *Incarnation*, in Hardy, *Christology of the Later Fathers*, 12–13.

38. Athanasius, *Incarnation*, in Hardy, *Christology of the Later Fathers*, 3.

39. Athanasius, *Incarnation*, in Hardy, *Christology of the Later Fathers*, 6.

40. Athanasius, *Incarnation*, in Hardy, *Christology of the Later Fathers*, 6.

alone. Nonetheless, the children of Adam are bound up in the consequences of Adam's sin—corruption and death.

Athanasius's focus on corruption and death is vividly seen against his understanding of personal sin and guilt. If salvation were merely a matter of legal guilt, he argues, repentance would be sufficient;[41] but the problem runs deeper. Somehow, human nature has to be restored and healed from the ravages of death. In a telling passage, Athanasius notes that even sinlessness cannot overcome humanity's inherent ontological corruption. Holy men such as Jeremiah and John, he writes, had been "hallowed from the womb" and were thus "holy and clean from all sin . . . nevertheless 'death reigned from Adam to Moses even over those that had not sinned after the similitude of Adam's transgression'; and thus man remained mortal and corruptible as before, liable to the affection proper to their nature."[42] Both Jeremiah and John, despite their impeccable *personal* holiness and guiltlessness, were inheritors of Adamic corruption and death. As such, they, too, stood in need of Christ's redemption.

Two aspects of Athanasius's framework on original sin are notable here. First, Athanasius distinguishes between volitional sin and ontological corruption. Athanasius is not the only church father to make this distinction (Augustine does so as well, as do the other orthodox teachers of the church). Volitional sin is an *act* that gives birth to, and arises out of, one's ontological corruption. One can, by a miracle of grace, be kept perfectly free from volitional sin (like Jeremiah and John), while yet being ontologically corrupted. Unusual, to be sure, but possible. Guilt, for Athanasius, is associated with volitional sin, not ontological corruption. This distinction helps us understand the second notable aspect of Athanasius's doctrine of original sin.

Insofar as guilt is associated with volitional sin rather than corruption, Athanasius offers us a framework of original sin as inherited corruption but not as inherited guilt. As we saw with Irenaeus, Adam's sin is Adam's alone. As such, Adam's guilt is Adam's alone. But this distance from Adam's guilt does not mean that humanity is untouched by Adam's failure. The effort to distance humanity entirely away from Adam's sin is a Pelagian overreach. True, Adam's posterity is not guilty of Adam's sin. But Adam's posterity is not untouched by it either. For Athanasius, all human beings are born into Adam's failure and his subsequent corruption; we are damaged, at the core of our being, by a sin we are not guilty of committing.

41. Athanasius, *Incarnation*, in Hardy, *Christology of the Later Fathers*, 7.
42. Athanasius, *Third Arian Discourse*, in NPNF2, 26.33.

C. Saint Cyril on the Inevitability of Personal Sin

Our tour of Eastern Orthodoxy concludes with Saint Cyril of Alexandria. Athanasius's idea that some holy people are born free of personal sin—and remain as such—should not lead us to think that the East has an overly rosy picture of human potential. Nor should it lead us to believe that humans are free of guilt. For the East, being volitionally sinless from birth is a unique and unusual miracle of grace. In nearly all cases, human beings are born into Adam's corruption in such a way that personal sins and guilt naturally and inevitably arise.

In a logic parallel to what we saw in Augustine, Cyril contends that humanity's inheritance of Adam's corruption creates an inevitable context for individual personal sin and guilt. He writes,

> Adam was created for incorruptibility and for life; in paradise he led a holy life: his mind was wholly devoted to the contemplation of God, his body was safe and peaceful, without the occurrence of any evil pleasure; the tumult of foolish propensities was non-existent within him; but when, due to sin, he fell into corruption, then pleasures and impurity penetrated his fleshly nature; the law of savagery appeared in our members. Nature became ill from sin by the disobedience of one man, that is from Adam. Thus was the multitude brought forth in sin; not that they shared in the error of Adam—they did not yet exist—but because they shared his nature, fallen under the law of sin. Accordingly . . . in Adam [human] nature became ill from corruption through disobedience, since the passions entered into it.[43]

Adam's one personal sin, for which he alone is guilty, poisoned the river of human life. Those drinking downstream from Adam's polluted morality inevitably become morally sick themselves. And made sick by Adam's sin, we cannot help spewing up our own personal acts of sins. The entire story of humanity is the story of each person adding his or her own personal sin and guilt to the headwaters of Adam's sin and guilt, until the river of sin and guilt has become a mighty torrent sweeping all before it.

For Cyril, Adam's sin leads to corruption, which leads to personal sin, which leads to personal guilt. Eastern Orthodox theologian Andrew Louth summarizes Cyril's (and the East's) basic logic of sin: "The consequences of my sin mingle with the consequences of others' sin, and the whole combines

---

43. Cyril, *Commentary on Romans*, 5.18, as quoted in Bobrinskoy, "Adamic Heritage," 35.

to form a kind of deafening cacophony."[44] Adam's corruption inevitably and naturally (apart from a miracle of grace) leads all human beings into their own personal sin and guilt.

III. Original Sin and Racism: East and West

We return now to Jim Wallis and his connection between racism and original sin. Wallis, in linking racism to original sin, is consciously and explicitly intending to implicate all white people in the sin of racism. He does not want to leave room for white folks to say, "Racism is bad, but I'm above it." For Wallis, the sin of racism has been passed from generation to generation, just like original sin has been passed from Adam to his posterity. Just as we cannot get free from Adam's sin without repentance, white people are born into a culture corrupted by inherited racism and cannot get free of it without repentance.

In my estimation, Wallis's use of original sin as a metaphor for American racism is effective but is hampered by his use of the Western Augustinian version of the doctrine. The Eastern Orthodox articulation, I believe, provides a more effective analogy. I offer the following thoughts about the usefulness and limits of the Western doctrine, as well as the benefits of the Eastern.

A. Inherited Corruption:
Where the Western Analogy Is Helpful

In my mind, Wallis's assumed Western Augustinian notion of original sin works well as a theological metaphor to illustrate his basic premise that the corruption of racism is passed from one generation to another. Even quite apart from Augustine's ontological realism, our experience confirms the reality of sin's transmission from generation to generation. The young boy raised by an alcoholic father will carry his father's dysfunction into adulthood; the young girl raised by an emotionally grasping mother will carry her mother's dysfunction into adulthood. Apart from a miracle of grace, the sins of the parents are passed on to and enacted by the children. And if not the exact sin, then some other expression of the same underlying dysfunction. Scripture, history, and the social sciences all confirm this. If the transmission of sin is true at the local level with respect to one's parents (and it is), and if it is true at the global level with respect to Adam and Eve (and it is), why could it not also be true at the cultural and national level with respect to racism?

---

44. Louth, *Introducing Eastern Orthodox Theology*, 72.

Theologian Willie Jennings, in his book *The Christian Imagination: Theology and the Origins of Race*, employs a logic similar to Wallis's. Jennings speaks of racism as a product of the Western world's "diseased social imagination"—an imagination rooted in colonization and the transatlantic slave trade.[45] Within the framework of this diseased social imagination, white pigmentation and Euro facial features (and thus Europeans) came to be viewed as superior to all other non-Euro skin pigmentations and facial features. As such, western Europeans felt legally and morally justified in enslaving nonwhites (who were conceived in subhuman terms). This diseased social imagination was an active feature in the days of America's founding and was consequently operative in crafting the original structures of America's formal racism—most especially its institution of race-based slavery. For Jennings, this diseased social imagination has been passed from generation to generation. Even after America put an end to formalized slavery, the diseased social imagination lingered on. The era of failed Reconstruction, lynching, Jim Crow, racialized segregation, redlining, and police brutality all reveal that the diseased social imagination continued even after America's original sin of slavery had ended.

And this diseased imagination touches all of us. Even the white seven-year-old Midwestern farm girl cannot escape the deeply engrained diseased imagination of the Western world. Her entire cultural world—consisting of her media, education, history, family, relationships (and even her religion!)—came of age in a problematically racialized world. She will need to be consciously counter-formed to resist her culture's inherent racial corruption, lest she be carried away by its racist currents.

I recognize that many of my fellow theological conservatives resist the notion that the corruption of racism passes from generation to generation in a way analogous to the corruption of original sin. But how could it not? The doctrine of original sin, so (rightly, in my mind) cherished by the conservative theological tradition, provides a ready framework for affirming the idea that sins are passed down from one generation to another. This is all the more true as we consider suprapersonal sins that go beyond individual personal choices and actions—sins such as racism, xenophobia, sexism, and classism.[46] Such sins extend to wrongful dispositions and states of being. They inform one's conceptions of worth, value, beauty, and what constitutes the good. For example, the misogyny of the misogynist can't be reduced to a simple list of harmful discrete actions; something in the misogynist's worldview regarding women is misshapen. Therefore, repentance for the misogynist will involve more than

---

45. Jennings, *Christian Imagination*, 6.

46. I am indebted to Ty Kieser and Daniel Lee Hill for their helpful analysis of suprapersonal and social sin. See their "Social Sin."

simply acknowledging sinful misogynistic actions but will necessarily involve acknowledging—and then reforming—the misogynist's entire way of considering women. This is the Augustinian doctrine of original sin. Not that we are thoroughly depraved in every possible way, but that our very state of being, our dispositions, and our life orientations have been misshapen by Adam's corruption. The Augustinian conception of inherited corruption reminds us that we have all been swallowed whole not only by Adam's *sin* but, even more desperately, by Adam's suprapersonal *sinfulness*. Inevitably, the structures and systems that are constructed by the collective aggregate of such suprapersonal sinfulness will invariably result in harm (to self and others). Misogynist states of being—not merely misogynist actions—create misogynist systems of oppression, which in turn reinforce and instigate further misogynist actions. The same pernicious circularity is true for racism.

Theological conservatives, even more so than theological liberals, should be quick to understand how America's racist founding infected not only our founding fathers but also their posterity with suprapersonal sin. It is a Pelagian-like error to deny the cultural transmission of racism from one generation to another or to suggest that each generation steps into the world *posse non peccare*—able not to sin, free and untainted by the deep cultural racism that came before.

So far, so good (so to speak), for Wallis's connection between racism and original sin. But it's at this point that the limits of the Augustinian approach begin to emerge.

For Wallis, the connection between racism and original sin provides justification for his call to repentance. "Sin must be named, exposed, and understood before it can be repented of."[47] The only way forward, Wallis contends, is for white people to repent of the guilt they have inherited from their white founding fathers. Nearly all Christians will agree with Wallis that sin must be named and repented of. But my own experience is that race conversations stall out when the language of repentance and guilt is introduced. Theological conservatives (and cultural conservatives, more generally) tend to react against the connection between racism and original sin precisely because of the inherited guilt that Wallis's Augustinian approach implies.

Many white Christians (perhaps even most) will (to varying degrees) acknowledge the tragic history of race in America. But most white conservatives resist accepting blame for a historical past (e.g., slavery) of which they had no part. Wallis says as much. "Over and over, I hear defensive white reactions such as 'I never owned slaves,' or . . . '*My* immigrant forefathers and mothers

---

47. Wallis, *America's Original Sin*, 35; italics in original.

came long after slavery was abolished. Why am I to blame for racism?"[48] For white conservative Christians, the egregious sins of slavery and open racism were committed upstream from them, and they feel it is unfair that they are being called to repent of something their forefathers did.

Indeed, my own experience in race conversations is that white people become increasingly less willing to acknowledge the tragedy of America's racial past the more that racial past is pinned on them. In the language of original sin, the white person says, "If you make me own inherited guilt (i.e., hold me culpable for the sins of past generations), I will refuse to own my inherited corruption (i.e., my diseased social imagination regarding race) even though I know it to be there. If you make me own both together, I'll just deny both together."

What is to be done? Some folks, like Wallis, are inclined to double down on the connection between racism and the Augustinian notion of inherited guilt: white people need to repent for the sins of their fathers. That's all there is to it. And until they are willing to do so, they cannot be free of the guilt of America's original sin.

B. Where the Eastern Analogy Is More Helpful

I agree with Wallis that racism has been transmitted from one generation to another in a way that is parallel to the transmission of original sin. And I agree with Jennings that the Western world has been steeped in a diseased social imagination regarding race. But how might Wallis's and Jennings's insights play out in an Eastern Orthodox framework? Three significant differences between East and West come to mind, drawn from the preceding survey of the Eastern doctrine of original sin.

Varying levels of culpability

As we saw in Irenaeus, the Eastern doctrine of the fall acknowledges varying levels of culpability for sin. For the East, the devil's sin was more destructive than Adam's. Sin is sin, of course, insofar as it separates us from the life of God. But not all sins have the same destructive power nor garner the same divine response. Those with greater power who sin against those with lesser power commit the more egregious and destructive sin, and thus incur the greater guilt. This insight regarding varying levels of culpability is helpful for race conversations.

48. Wallis, *America's Original Sin*, 35.

All Americans are implicated in the racism of the West's diseased imagination. But not all equally. Not every American is a Klan member. The white seven-year-old Midwestern farm girl who plays happily with her adopted cousin from Ethiopia may be infected with the West's diseased imagination; but at such a tender age, she is as much a victim as a perpetrator of racism. The level of repentance required of her at the age of seven is (far!) less than what will be required of her if she grows up to be an active Klan member. The Eastern doctrine of original sin teaches us that all of us have been harmed by sin and that all sin must be named and owned; but it also teaches us that not all sins are as deeply engrained or damaging.

By way of analogy (if the reader will pardon my use of an analogy to justify the usefulness of an analogy), I was discussing the merits of Christian theology with my Buddhist neighbor. My neighbor had been raised Roman Catholic but rejected the faith because he found Christianity far too negative in its view of human nature (he had grown up with a good dose of Augustinian anthropology). As we talked about sin and its universal impact, he reacted very strongly against Christianity. It occurred to me that what he was hearing and what I was saying weren't the same things. When I said, "Christianity teaches that all humans are sinners," what he heard was "Christianity teaches that all humans are like the orcs in Tolkien's *Lord of the Rings*—deformed subhumans worthy only of destruction." That wasn't what I was saying, but my neighbor had been reared in a context where sin was spoken of in such totalizing ways that he didn't have a category for varying degrees of culpability. And since he wasn't ready to admit to being an orc, he rejected Christianity all together. The same thing can happen in race conversations. If we fail to account for varying levels of culpability, if we (aggressively) speak of racism in totalizing ways that lack nuance, we may end up causing many white folks to reject race conversations all together.

When Christians on the theological left say "All white people are racists," they typically don't mean anything more or less than what Christians on the theological right mean when they say "All people are sinners." Both statements intend to communicate the basic truth that sin and racism touch us all; no one is exempt. But neither statement is intended to mean that sin and racism touch us all equally. Folks on the left don't generally mean to say that all white people are (to use Augustine's language) a "mass of racism, totally vitiated, morally equivalent to a Klan member, damned, and damnable." But this is what many white conservatives hear. And the white response to the Augustinian overreach is an essentially Pelagian denial of any culpability whatsoever regarding racism. The Eastern doctrine of original sin offers a more balanced (and accurate) analogy for speaking about the variegated culpability associated with racism.

Inherited corruption without inherited guilt

The Western doctrine of original sin implicates humans in both inherited corruption and guilt. But as we saw in Athanasius, the Eastern doctrine implicates us only in inherited corruption. We are guilty for our own personal sins, to be sure, and are called to repent of them. But we are not called to repent of Adam's sin. By the same logic, white Americans have inherited the racial corruption of America's founders but not the guilt of America's founders. The guilt of white people regarding racism is their own.

And I wonder if the Eastern focus on inherited corruption is what Wallis is really after in the end. Notably, in his response to white evasions of Augustinian guilt, he answers with Eastern Orthodox corruption. When white people tell him that they are not guilty of slavery, he responds by asserting the realities of racial corruption: "implicit bias" and "white privilege."[49] Well and good. But contemporary implicit bias and white privilege are not the cause of America's past slavery; rather, America's past slavery (and the diseased social imagination) is the cause of today's implicit bias and white privilege. I can truthfully affirm the reality of my racialized corruption (i.e., my implicit bias and white privilege) without having to, in the same breath, accept guilt for the slavery of my fathers.

It's important to note, however, that my lack of personal guilt for the past racial crimes of my American forefathers does not excuse me from the inevitable responsibility I have of helping to clean up the mess that has been handed down to me and that I have been complicit in helping to propagate. I may not be responsible before God for the sins of my fathers; but insofar as those sins continue to linger in myself and the world, I am responsible before God to help heal the damage done by them. This is the East's message of the church's engagement with the sinful world. Father Alexander Schmemann, an orthodox priest and liturgical theologian, writes of how the world needs someone to "stand in the center" of the world's chaos and offer a cup of joy, of beauty, and of wisdom. "This 'someone' is Christ," Schmemann says. Jesus is "the new Adam who restores that 'Eucharistic life' which I, the old Adam have rejected and lost; who makes me again what I am, and restores the world to me. And if the Church *is in Christ*, its initial act is always . . . returning the

---

49. Wallis, *America's Original Sin*, 34; italics in original.

world to God."[50] The mission of the church is to return the world to God and to unmake the ravages of Adam's sin.

Thus, the grace of Christ works in both personal and corporate ways. Christ heals us from the ravages of our racialized corruption and forgives our personal racial sins, and he empowers us to help heal a racialized and broken world that (in the words of Louth again) "was already laid waste long before we came along."[51]

The inevitability of personal guilt

And finally, Saint Cyril reminds us that our inherited corruption inevitably manifests itself in personal volitional sin. Even though the Eastern account of sin does not require me to own the guilt of my forefathers' racism, this does not mean that I am thereby innocent of the guilt of racism. The racism of my national forefathers has shaped an entire racist culture, which has in turn shaped my own expectations and views of race. I have been born into a diseased social imagination, and I have not been unscathed by it. Indeed, I have even benefited from it (with respect to worldly power, opportunities, and status). This diseased social imagination will, at some level, give birth to racism in my actions—even if that racism consists only of sins of omission or the passive indulgence of the inequities created by America's historical racism, without regard for how those inequities have harmed and continue to harm racial minorities. Insofar as I have personally lived into, supported, and acted out the racist tendencies and structures of my culture, I am guilty of racism and must repent of it.

Analogously, all human beings enter the world with a share of Adam's sexual brokenness. Even the best instances of a deep and genuine Christian social upbringing will not prevent a person from inevitably acting out some expression of this sexual brokenness. Not all of us (thank God) will be addicted to pornography, have affairs, or live rapacious and sexually predatory lives. But it is a Pelagian error (and simply untrue) to presume that our sexual brokenness (i.e., our inherited sexual corruption) will have no expression in our actions or thought life. In the same way, our inherited racial brokenness will inevitably manifest itself in some expression of racial sin.

Only by God's grace and repentance are we healed from the sins of our biological parents. Only by God's grace and repentance are we healed from the sins of Adam and Eve. And only by God's grace and repentance are we healed

---

50. Schmemann, *For the Life of the World*, 75.

51. Louth, *Introducing Eastern Orthodox Theology*, 73.

from the sins of American culture. And by God's grace given freely in Christ, we can be, and are, healed.

IV. Conclusion

Those on the theological left (like Wallis) who want to use the doctrine of original sin as an analogy to inform conversations about race do better to work from the Eastern Orthodox version of the doctrine, with its emphasis on inherited corruption, rather than the Western alternative, with its emphasis on inherited guilt. The strength of the Augustinian approach is its totalizing power. It does not allow anyone to escape its accusing judgment. When used as an analogy for America's racism, it ably makes the point that racism has infected all of us, and therefore all need to repent. But its strength is also its weakness. It is too ham-fisted; it overreaches insofar as it lays the guilt of America's forefathers on their posterity. The Eastern Orthodox logic allows for more nuance. While it likewise implicates everyone in the corruption of America's founding racism, it calls for repentance related only to one's own sins.

In the same way, those on the theological right who reflexively reject the analogy between racism and original sin do well to consider how the logic of the Eastern Orthodox emphasis on inherited corruption challenges their too optimistic assertions that they "have nothing to do" with America's racist past. The Eastern Orthodox articulation provides helpful insight about the lingering effects of generational racism and how those lingering effects inevitably lead all of us into some measure of our own personal expressions of racism and bigotry.

The good news—the best news!—about the connection between racism and original sin (East and West) is that God forgives all sin. What's more, he heals all sin in Christ. Perhaps not perfectly and fully this side of the resurrection, but nonetheless truly and meaningfully. May God, in his kindness, send the Stronger Man to free us from the racist tyranny of the strong man. May he open our eyes to see our own inherited racial corruption, give us the gift of repentance for our racial sins, and empower us to return the life of God to a broken and racialized world.

Bibliography

Anatolios, Khaled. *Athanasius: The Coherence of His Thought.* New York: Routledge, 1998.
Augustine. *The Literal Meaning of Genesis, Vol. 1.* Ancient Christian Writers 41. Mahwah, NJ: Paulist, 1982.

Bobrinskoy, Boris. "The Adamic Heritage According to Fr. John Meyendorff." *St. Vladimir's Quarterly* 42 (1998) 33–44.

Coxe, Cleveland A., ed. *The Apostolic Fathers with Justin Martyr and Irenaeus.* Ante-Nicene Fathers 1. 1885. Reprint, Peabody, MA: Hendrickson, 2004.

DeYoung, Kevin. "Reparations: A Critical Theological Review." *The Gospel Coalition*, 22 Apr 2021. https://www.thegospelcoalition.org/blogs/kevin-deyoung/reparations-a-critical-theological-review/.

Hardy, Edward R. *The Christology of the Later Fathers.* Louisville: John Knox, 1954.

Hiestand, Gerald. "Irenaeus, the Devil, and the Goodness of Creation: How Irenaeus' Account of the Devil Reshapes the Christian Narrative in a Pro-Terrestrial Direction." In *Creation and Doxology: The Beginning and End of God's Good World*, edited by Gerald Hiestand and Todd Wilson, 99–117. Downers Grove, IL: IVP Academic, 2018.

Jennings, Willie. *The Christian Imagination.* New Haven: Yale University Press, 2010.

Kieser, Ty, and Daniel Lee Hill. "Social Sin and the Sinless Savior: Delineating Supra-Personal Sin in Continuity with Conciliar Christology." In *Modern Theology* (forthcoming).

Louth, Andrew. *Introducing Eastern Orthodox Theology.* Downers Grove, IL: IVP Academic, 2013.

MacKenzie, Iain. M. *Irenaeus's Demonstration of the Apostolic Preaching: A Theological Commentary.* Burlington, VT: Ashgate, 2002.

McGiffert, Arthur Cushman. *A History of Christian Thought.* New York: Scribner's Sons, 1933.

Portalie, Eugene. *A Guide to the Thought of Saint Augustine.* Chicago: Regnery, 1960.

Schmemann, Alexander. *For the Life of the World.* Yonkers, NY: St. Vladimir Seminary Press, 2018.

Steenberg, Matthew. "Children in Paradise: Adam and Eve as 'Infant' in Irenaeus of Lyons." *Journal of Early Christian Studies* 12 (Spring 2004) 1–22.

TeSelle, Eugene. *Augustine the Theologian.* Eugene, OR: Wipf & Stock, 2002.

Wallis, Jim. "America's Original Sin." *Sojourners*, Nov 1987. https://sojo.net/magazine/november-1987/americas-original-sin.

———. *America's Original Sin: Racism, White Privilege, and the Bridge to a New America.* Grand Rapids: Brazos, 2016.

Part Three

CONTEXTUAL THEOLOGY

9

The Latino Church

A Story of Complexity and Its Challenges Today

PAUL SANCHEZ

THE HISTORY OF LATINO culture is surprisingly complex. It is a story of conquest, protest, evolution, and perseverance—*fusión, mestizaje,* and life in *la
frontera.* Formed within a culture infused with faith, the Latino church in the
United States embodies this complexity, and though faced with challenges, it
offers insights for the broader family of Evangelicals who themselves are in a
time of soul-searching.[1]

My interest in this topic is based in my personal background as well as
years of ministry and intent observation. As the name Sanchez suggests, I
have a Hispanic heritage. My grandfather immigrated to the United States in
search of a better life, and his children were born as American citizens. But he
later sent two of his children back to Mexico, where my father spent the most
formative years of his adolescence living with his *primos* who became like
siblings. Through my childhood, there were regular visits to and from family
across the border, and the time I spent in Mexico City left a deep impression

---

1. For sources on the questions facing Evangelicals today, especially related to the essence of evangelical identity, see Kidd, *Who Is an Evangelical?*, and Noll et al., *Evangelicals.*

on me. San José, California, where I was born and raised, has no ethnic majority, but Hispanics or Latinos represent the largest ethnic group. The city has a a rich mixture of more recent Hispanic immigrants from Latin America, as well as an established Chicano culture that is a hybrid of Mexican culture and urban American culture.[2] Growing up in a multiethnic Pentecostal church, I was taught that there were other Christians out there, but as people of the Spirit we had a special connection to God, especially compared to my Roman Catholic family in Mexico and the many nominal Catholics who lived around us. My father's love of history ensured that I was aware of the religious history that had been the basis for California's establishment in the eighteenth century. A freeway in the heart of our city was named for Franciscan missionary Junípero Serra who has been called California's founding father on account of the missions he established, which to this day define California's urban geography. Walking the grounds of one of Serra's missions was no less moving for me than visiting the grand cathedral at Zócalo in Mexico City.[3] This mixture of passionate Pentecostal Evangelicalism and Roman Catholic heritage provided an intriguing environment for someone who would one day become a church historian.

After being away from California for years of education in the Midwest and southeastern United States, I returned to my hometown to pastor a church in the urban core in Eastside San José. Serving a majority Latino and bilingual church became another opportunity to reflect on the story of Latino Christianity in the United States. Many of the observations I had made over the years were reaffirmed but also deepened by this experience. And new observations and challenges offered greater insight as I served a church and community that was as foreign to most of my fellow Southern Baptists as an international missions post might be. While pastoring, I began working with Southern Baptist Theological Seminary's Online Hispanic Program (OHP), which has allowed me to teach students from across Latin America. Interacting with them has been deeply enriching and has provided a new opportunity to learn as I participate in this remarkable expansion of theological education for Latino Evangelicals. Seeing the zeal of these men and women, as well as those I have taught on the ground in Guatemala and Ecuador, gives me great

2. The term *Chicano* was first used during the Civil Rights movement to describe Latinos, and especially people of Mexican heritage, in California and the Southwest. As organized movements emerged and gained media attention, journalists called them Chicanos. Not initially receiving universal approval by Hispanics themselves, the term eventually came into popular use and today is used widely by Mexican Americans. See Acuña, *Occupied America*.

3. For sources on Junípero Serra, see Hackel, *Junípero Serra*, and Couve de Murville, *Man Who Founded California*.

hope for the future of the Latino church and, with it, hope for the broader evangelical family.

It was in Ecuador that I visited the ruins of Ingapirca, high in the mountains in the Cañar Province. They are the more extensive Incan ruins in Ecuador, and they are astonishing for the skill and intentionality that they evidence. The Incas were the Romans of South America. The sheer size and sophistication of their empire was extraordinary.[4] In this region where we spent a week teaching pastors, most of the people still speak an indigenous language that preceded Spanish colonization. Quechua is their heart language. Theirs is a rich indigenous culture with relatively few *mestizos*, unlike the population in most Latin American cities.[5] But as a historian, I found myself reflecting on the complexity of the region's history. I recognized that it had been only a matter of decades before the Spanish arrived that the Incas colonized the region that had been controlled by the Cañari.[6] The Cañari themselves were a powerful and ambitious people before they succumbed to the imperial ambitions of the Incas. With great determination, the Cañari resisted the Incas for years, until the 1470s, when through a mixture of conquest and diplomacy, the Incas became their colonial overlords. Still considering the Incas to be invaders when the Spanish arrived in 1534, the Cañari allied with the Spanish against the Inca, which helped seal Spanish victory on the continent and made way for centuries of Spanish colonization.[7]

Reflecting on this history, I was struck to discover that the Quechua language itself came from the Incas and not the Cañari. So, the indigenous language that forms a central part of their heritage was actually a product of conquest before a greater power—the Spanish—also conquered the region and left their own imprint. As we peel back the onion of Latino history, we find a complex story that is centuries of cultural evolution in the making. If the larger story of Hispanic culture is complex, the story of Latino religion in the United States is likewise so. In this exploration, I focus on evangelical Protestants, but when talking about Latino culture, Roman Catholicism is never far removed. It is a complex story, but it provides an opportunity for the kind of reflection that is good for the church, especially as Evangelicals are asking deep questions about the state and future of the movement.

4. For a source on the Incas, see D'Altroy, *Incas*.

5. *Mestizo* is a Spanish term which means mixed ethnicity and is widely used to describe the great majority of Latin America's population that has a mixed ancestry, part Spanish and part indigenous. The term *fusión* is used to refer to the mixing or fusion of cultures that formed Latino society, as opposed to biological mixing.

6. For a concise account of the Cañari, see Thornton, *Cultural History*. For a comprehensive study, see Guevara, *Identidad del Pueblo Cañari*.

7. See Hemming, *Conquest of the Incas*.

COMPLEXITY

The history of Latin America is full of color and fascination, but also trag-edy. The well-known church historian Justo González lays out this tangled story with remarkable candor. He argues that such candor stands in contrast to what is often a more whitewashed approach to the telling of history in the United States:

> Hispanics, on the other hand, have had to deal with a different sort of history. We always knew that our ancestors were not guilt-less. Our Spanish ancestors took the lands of our Indian ancestors. Some of our Indian ancestors practiced human sacrifice and can-nibalism. Some of our Spanish forefathers raped our Indian fore-mothers. Some of our Indian foremothers betrayed their people in favor of the invaders. It is not a pretty story.[8]

González contends that the messiness of Latino history is not merely one point in a larger story but is a central part of the grand narrative. I will explore this more extensively in a subsequent section, but for now it is sufficient to reveal the messiness of Latino history, which provides an example of a people who formed a sense of identity, though it was built upon a broken past.

The history of Latinos in what is now the United States goes back several centuries. It is worth noting that the first Hispanics to enter the United States did not come as immigrants but were absorbed into a new country when the United States took possession of a vast area of the North American continent that had belonged to Mexico. What are now the states of California, Nevada, Arizona, Utah, New Mexico, and portions of others became part of the Union of the United States in 1848 at the conclusion of the Mexican-American War.[9] Justo González argues that it is more accurate to say that the United States migrated into Hispanic lands. To be sure, immigration is an important part of the Latino story, but not the whole story.[10] But immigration has had a forma-tive role in shaping Latino culture. Increasingly after World War II, it was principally Mexicans who began immigrating to the United States in large numbers, followed by Latinos from other countries. Their reasons are often economic; sometimes they are political or related to escalating violence in

---

8. González, *Mañana*, 40.

9. The Treaty of Guadalupe Hidalgo defined these lands as the spoils of war when the United States defeated Mexico. To this day, this remains a sensitive subject to many Mexican citizens who consider the Mexican-American War an unjust war of conquest and the seizing of Mexican land a form of theft. For a history of the Mexican-American War, see Guardino, *Dead March*.

10. González, *Mañana*, 31–33.

their homeland. Regardless of their motivations, Latinos come to this new land as exiles. González perfectly captures how the journey northward shapes the Latino mind: "If . . . the lands of our birth are now permanently lost to us, if we no longer hope to return but have cast our lot in this adoptive land, we are no longer Latin Americans living in exile in the United States, but Hispanic Americans, people who have no other land than this, but who nevertheless remain exiles."[11] The second and subsequent generations do not feel this in the same measure, but there often remains a lingering uneasiness in a society that can make brown-skinned Americans feel like perpetual immigrants. Like the previous point about the messiness of Latino history, the exile experience of Latinos offers yet another insight that might serve Evangelicals more broadly.

Considering another angle for complexity, Latino ethnicity itself proves to be literally complex. A key term for this is *mestizaje*, which refers to the ethnic mixture that occurred broadly in Latin American countries.[12] Although it varies from country to country, region to region, most Hispanics today are of mixed ancestry: Spanish, indigenous, as well as African and other ethnicities. Reies López Tijerina was a civil rights activist in New Mexico who, like the better-known Cesar Chavez, helped galvanize a movement for equal rights for Hispanic Americans. When the term *Chicano* was first being used, Tijerina argued that the term *Indo-Hispano* better captured the essence of Latino ethnicity and culture, since the Spanish represented a sort of "father," and the Indians represented a "mother." Both "parents" were essential for what it means to be Latino.[13] Although the term failed to garner wide use, it captures well the cultural *mestizaje* that is essential to Latino history and identity. Although most Latin Americans are *mestizo*, significant variation exists, and with this are observable correlations associated with class, privilege, and, consequentially with prejudice, related to the relative percentage of indigenous versus European ancestry. This topic is no less provocative to Latin Americans than questions related to racism are to the people of the United States, and it serves as a reminder that the problem of ethnic prejudice is not unique to the United States.

Additionally, religion has been essential to Latino culture and history. From the beginning, the Roman Catholic faith of the Spanish crown was inextricably linked to the colonial mission in the new world. Roman Catholicism has been entwined with Hispanic culture for more than five centuries, which means that any consideration of religion in Latino history has some

11. González, *Mañana*, 41.

12. The common word *mestizo* is the adjective form of the noun *mestizaje*, which means mixing.

13. For a source on Tijerina, see Oropeza, *King of the Adobe*.

connection to Catholic religion. Evangelical Protestantism emerged as a genuine movement in Latin America in the nineteenth century. Most notably with the rise of Pentecostalism in the early twentieth, various traditions of Evangelical Christianity grew and sometimes did so with impressive multiplicity. Today, Evangelicals rival Roman Catholics in several regions of Latin America. In the United States, evangelical churches grew steadily in the twentieth century. They did so through conversions as well as Protestant immigration from Latin America. A large portion of Latino Protestants are Pentecostal or charismatic, but there are also large numbers of Baptists, along with Methodists, and many independent evangelical churches that roughly equate with American "Bible" churches. Today, Latino Evangelicals represent a large and dynamic subgroup of American Evangelicalism. But the majority of Latinos remain Roman Catholic, and the influence of the Roman church on Hispanic American culture continues to be strong, which is the source of one of the challenges to be considered below.[14]

Now, with a better grasp on the complexity of this story, I will explore a series of challenges that face the Latino church today and will provide insights that I hope can serve Evangelicals both within but also beyond the Latino community.

CHALLENGES

Latino churches represent a growing and now substantial part of Evangelical Christianity in the United States, but they are not without significant challenges. Some of these are shared by churches of other minority groups, but Latinos' own history has also resulted in particular obstacles to be overcome.

The first of these relates directly to Protestant Evangelicalism itself. For Latinos, leaving Roman Catholicism to become a Protestant often involves a significant level of separation from one's family and culture. After more than five centuries, Hispanic culture is entwined with Roman Catholicism.[15] As a result, there is a common perception that leaving Roman Catholicism is tantamount to rejecting Hispanic culture. For many Latinos, embracing the evangelical gospel and joining with the evangelical community can alienate believers from their families. And in a culture that is so strongly oriented toward family, this can be a heavy burden to bear. Being excluded from invitations to birthday parties, holidays, or other family gatherings is painful.

14. For the history of Christianity in Latin America, see González and González, *Christianity in Latin America*, and Orique et al., *Oxford Handbook*. For a survey of Latin American evangelical theology, see Salinas, *Taking Up the Mantle*.

15. González, *Mañana*, 55–66.

Reluctant invitations are marginally better but might still mean receiving the cold shoulder from some family members. The point is not that this never happens to white Americans, African Americans, or others, but it is often accentuated for Latinos because of the close identity of the Roman faith with their culture. In this environment, the cost to follow Christ is felt in a tangible way. But there is a positive side to this. When people face a level of alienation from their biological family, they are often eager to make the local church their new family. I witnessed this at the church I pastored in San José, where the fellowship of the church was anything but superficial. In a short time, the church truly became like family to me, my wife, and my children, and in a way that we have never experienced elsewhere. And yet, Latino churches have to reckon with this challenge as they seek to make disciples in their communities.

Another challenge is the product of the generational dynamics of Latino immigration. Once established in the United States, a stunning evolution occurs as the first generation gives way to the second. In what almost seems like an overnight phenomenon, the second and subsequent generations of Latinos become cultural hybrids, not fully belonging to their parents' culture nor entirely to the American culture around them. In his book *A Future for the Latino Church*, Daniel Rodriguez describes well this fascinating evolution. Drawing from his own story, he describes how children become Mexican-American—something that is neither fully Mexican nor generically American. With great insight, he captures this experience of "living in the hyphen."[16] With the differences that emerge between the first and subsequent generations, churches face a series of dilemmas if they will continue to worship together as a single church. Some issues are matters of style and taste, which have a range of relative importance, but one question turns out to be essential as churches decide which language they will use for worship. Will they worship in Spanish or English, or will they try to incorporate both? This generational struggle plays out in other immigrant churches too. When I wrestled with these questions as a pastor, I formed a bond with a fellow pastor who served a Chinese church that faced nearly identical generational dynamics. The second generation prefers to worship in English, but that does not mean they feel at home in majority-white churches either. This is an expression of "living in the hyphen." Rodriguez says, "While we often feel rejected by the foreign-born for being *agringado* (Americanized), we also perceive that we are treated as second-class citizens in the country of our birth and often treated as 'outsiders' in the churches of the dominant group."[17] The majority

16. Rodriguez, *Future for the Latino Church*, 22–23, 35.

17. Rodriguez, *Future for the Latino Church*, 35. Rodriguez draws parallels from the New Testament in Acts 6 when two cultures existed together in the church—the Hellenists

of Latinos in the United States born in this country are English-dominant and imbibe much of American culture, but they remain Latinos at heart, with tastes and values that are distinct from the majority culture.[18] Latino churches face the challenge of navigating this complex cultural landscape, but in an age of globalization, these sorts of challenges will increasingly be a part of the evangelical landscape.

A different kind of challenge has been the growth of sociopolitical ideologies that are antagonistic toward Christianity. In his book *Brown Church*, Robert Chao Romero describes the shock that many Hispanic Christians experience when they make their way to college and are told that Christianity is a "white man's religion." In this climate, Christianity is said to be inherently oppressive, especially to people of color, or at the very least unhelpful in answering the most pressing issues of today. Evangelicalism in particular is singled out as a fundamentally political movement that leverages racism and xenophobia for its ends.[19] Latinos, of course, are not alone in this. Others, like African Americans, face the same kinds of rhetoric. A few years ago, when I was teaching a course in church history for Gateway Seminary in California, an African American student shared that people at work took issue with his Christian faith. How could a self-respecting black man profess a faith that once propped up chattel slavery and colonialism? The student expressed how helpful it had been to be in the class, to have answers for his own faith but also for people in his community. The burden of confronting these challenges has increased in recent years, and one can expect that this will only continue.

A final challenge relates to racism and prejudice. There are four angles to this. The most obvious is the marginalization of Hispanic people in American society. All immigrants face some measure of this, but a complex history with Latin America and the effects of racialization have intensified this challenge for Latinos. One result is that Hispanic churches and ministries have often had to make do with minimal resources.

As another angle, generational dynamics can also provoke a form of prejudice. Daniel Rodriguez describes how first-generation Latinos sometimes judge the second generation to be *pochos* or *agringados*, which are pejorative terms, especially for Mexican Americans, when they do not speak Spanish or are judged to be too Americanized.[20]

Racial prejudice from Latinos toward other groups also exists. Whether toward African Americans, white Americans, or others, this kind of prejudice

---

and Hebrews—both Jewish, but with significant cultural differences.

18. Rodriguez, *Future for the Latino Church*, 16, 37–42, 57.

19. Romero, *Brown Church*, 1–10. See also González, *Mañana*, 26, 110.

20. Rodriguez, *Future for the Latino Church*, 21, 59–62.

is a reminder of the universal effects of sinfulness upon the human heart. Robert Romero confronts the issue head-on: "As followers of Jesus, we condemn all racist attitudes and all forms of racial inequality that are found in the Latina/o community."[21]

Connected to this, there is within the Latino community a form of racial bias that relates to Latino diversity itself—the ethnic and cultural *mestizaje* of the Hispanic community. Especially in Latin America, physical traits that suggest a Spanish heritage come with a form of social privilege that sets some Latinos apart from others who exhibit a primarily indigenous ethnicity.

These are contentious issues in the Latino community, but like all sinful mindsets and attitudes, sins like partiality must be addressed as a part of Christian discipleship and kingdom proclamation, as matters of righteousness and justice.

Through all such challenges, the Latino church has found solace and guidance in the Scriptures and has maintained a vibrant faith and ecclesial community. I will conclude by offering some insights from the Latino church that I believe can serve the broader evangelical family.

INSIGHTS

The first insight goes back to the fundamental character of the Latino story itself. Justo González articulates what he calls the "non-innocence" view of history in his book *Mañana*, where he argues that Latinos have lived with an ugly history that, regardless of its complexity, "is not a pretty story."[22] But as a result, Latinos have learned to accept their story for what it is, without whitewashing even its ugliest aspects. González likens this to the way that the Bible is honest about the failures of even its most cherished heroes, like Moses, David, and Peter. The brokenness of Latino history has offered Latino believers, and might offer others, insight into how the biblical story, even through suffering, held forth hope until the coming of Christ and now does so until his second coming.[23] Christians should not be unwilling to acknowledge the troubled aspects of their history, including the more recent history of white Evangelicals who, at times, have been complicit in racism and, in some cases, were leading proponents of racial hierarchy.[24] As Evangelicals engage in soul-searching in our time, Latino history might provide an example, for instance,

---

21. Romero, *Brown Church*, 49.

22. González, *Mañana*, 40.

23. González, *Mañana*, 75–80.

24. See for example, Dupont, *Mississippi Praying*.

as Evangelicals consider whether to honor men like Jonathan Edwards and George Whitefield who were more than complicit in slavery. Latinos have tended to acknowledge the great deeds of historical figures while also speaking plainly about their sins. Latinos, González argues, have nothing to hide: "We have no skeletons in our closet. Our skeletons are at the very heart of our history and our reality as a people."[25] González argues that white Americans have had more difficulty acknowledging evil and injustice in their history, especially when it relates to their heroes. Latinos have learned to recognize the good or significant acts of men and women from the past, without exalting them uncritically. Latino history is messy, but when we get down to it, all history is messy, because in history, we tell the stories of sinful human beings.

Latinos know what it means to live as exiles. The Latino experience of colonization, immigration, and marginalization provides insight into one of the central themes of the Christian faith, that God's people are sojourners in this fallen world. Another group, African Americans, have certainly experienced their own history of marginalization and lived as exiles even in the land of their birth. In a review of Rod Dreher's widely popular *The Benedict Option*, Jemar Tisby, an African American scholar, perceptively critiques Dreher for overlooking the history of the black church as he theorized about how Christians might live in a future that includes significant social marginalization.[26] I believe the Latino experience adds another angle for Christians to consider as we face the likelihood of increasing hostility from American society. In a book titled *Borderlands/La Frontera: The New Mestiza*, Gloria Anzaldúa describes the Latino experience as one of living in *la frontera*—the borderlands. Robert Chao Romero applies this to religious life, as we have already discussed. If evangelical Christians are faced with social marginalization in the future, there is wisdom to be gained from Latinos and other marginalized groups who have endured such circumstances for generations. Beyond this, we find insight into the Christian faith itself. Christianity is a pilgrim's religion. Every Christian must recognize that we are sojourners who must learn to live well in this world while longing for another.

Beyond these insights, the story of Latino Christianity offers much more to be explored. As the United States and American Christianity become more diverse, it will be a great loss if mainstream Evangelicalism overlooks these stories. In addition to the history of Latino Christianity in the broadest sense, spirituality seems to be particularly ripe for study, especially when we consider

25. González, *Mañana*, 77–78.

26. Jemar Tisby's review is no longer available from its original source, which was the Reformed African American Network at raanetwork.org. However, a portion of it is still available. See Tisby, "Real Reason."

the impressive growth and influence of Pentecostalism in Latin America and among Latinos in the United States. And the role that spirituality played in the Hispanic wing of the civil rights movement is also a fascinating and largely overlooked topic for study.[27] If evangelical seminaries send out graduates with little to no exposure to the rich diversity of Christ's church in the United States, it will both impoverish Evangelicalism and also perpetuate the racial divisions that have long existed. I am hopeful that this brief opportunity for reflection on the Latino church will be a blessing for Evangelicals of every color and background and will further the hope for a unified mission to serve our one Lord, Jesus Christ.

BIBLIOGRAPHY

Acuña, Rodolfo. *Occupied America: A History of Chicanos*. 8th ed. New York: Pearson, 2007.

Anderson, Allan Heaton. *To the Ends of the Earth: Pentecostalism and the Transformation of World Christianity*. New York: Oxford University Press, 2013.

Anzaldúa, Gloria. *Borderlands/La Frontera: The New Mestiza*. 25th ed. San Francisco: Aunt Lute, 2012.

Aponte, Edwin D. *¡Santo! Varieties of Latino/a Spirituality*. Ossining, NY: Orbis, 2012.

Aponte, Edwin D., and Miguel De La Torre. *Introducing Latinx Theologies*. Ossining, NY: Orbis, 2020.

Barger, Lilian Calles. *The World Come of Age: An Intellectual History of Liberation Theology*. New York: Oxford University Press, 2018.

Couve de Murville, Maurice Noël Léon. *The Man Who Founded California: The Life of Blessed Junípero Serra*. San Francisco: Ignatius, 2000.

D'Altroy, Terence N. *The Incas*. 2nd ed. Malden, MA: Wiley-Blackwell, 2015.

Dupont, Carolyn Renée. *Mississippi Praying: Southern White Evangelicals and the Civil Rights Movement, 1945–1975*. New York: New York University Press, 2013.

González, Justo L. *Mañana: Christian Theology from a Hispanic Perspective*. Nashville: Abingdon, 1990.

González, Ondina E., and Justo L. González. *Christianity in Latin America: A History*. Cambridge: Cambridge University Press, 2008.

———. *Nuestra Fe: A Latin American Church History Sourcebook*. Nashville: Abingdon, 2014.

Guardino, Peter. *The Dead March: A History of the Mexican-American War*. Cambridge, MA: Harvard University Press, 2020.

Guevara, Hugo Burgos. *La Identidad del Pueblo Cañari: De-construcción de una Nación Étnica*. Quito: Abya Yala, 2003.

Hackel, Steven W. *Junípero Serra: California's Founding Father*. New York: Hill & Wang, 2013.

Hallenweger, Walter J. *Pentecostalism: Origins and Developments Worldwide*. Peabody, MA: Hendrickson, 1997.

27. Robert Romero references the spirituality of Cesar Chavez and the portion of the civil rights movement that he led (*Brown Church*, 120–22).

Hartch, Todd. *Mexico*. Understanding World Christianity 3. Minneapolis: Fortress, 2019.

Hemming, John. *The Conquest of the Incas*. Boston: Mariner, 2003.

Kidd, Thomas. *Who Is an Evangelical? The History of a Movement in Crisis*. New Haven: Yale University Press, 2019.

Martínez, Juan Francisco. *The Story of Latino Protestants in the United States*. Grand Rapids: Eerdmans, 2018.

Noll, Mark A., et al., eds. *Evangelicals: Who They Have Been, Are Now, and Could Be*. Grand Rapids: Eerdmans, 2019.

Orique, David Thomas, et al. *The Oxford Handbook of Latin American Christianity*. Oxford: Oxford University Press, 2020.

Oropeza, Lorena. *The King of the Adobe: Reies López Tijerina, Lost Prophet of the Chicano Movement*. Chapel Hill: University of North Carolina Press, 2019.

Rodriguez, Daniel A. *A Future for the Latino Church: Models for Multilingual, Multigenerational Hispanic Congregations*. Downers Grove, IL: IVP Academic, 2011.

Romero, Robert Chao. *Brown Church: Five Centuries of Latina/o Social Justice, Theology, and Identity*. Downers Grove, IL: IVP Academic, 2020.

Salinas, J. Daniel. *Taking Up the Mantle: Latin American Evangelical Theology in the 20th Century*. Cumbria, UK: Langham Global Library, 2017.

Sánchez, Daniel. *Hispanic Realities Impacting America: Implications for Evangelism & Missions*. Fort Worth, TX: Church Starting Network, 2006.

Steward, Julian H., ed. *The Andean Civilizations*. Vol. 2 of *Handbook of South American Indians*. 7 vols. Smithsonian Institution Bureau of American Ethnology. Washington, DC: Government, 1946.

Suárez, Federico González. *Estudio Historico Sober Los Cañaris, Antiguos Habitantes de la Providencia del Azuay en la Republica del Ecuador*. Quito: José Guzman Almeida, 1878.

Thornton, John K. *A Cultural History of the Atlantic World, 1250–1820*. Cambridge: Cambridge University Press, 2012.

Tisby, Jemar. "The Real Reason the Benedict Option Leaves Out the Black Church." *The Aquila Report*, 1 Apr 2017. https://theaquilareport.com/real-reason-benedict-option-leaves-black-church/.

Vargas, Zaragosa. *Crucible of Struggle: A History of Mexican Americans from Colonial Times to the Present Era*. 2nd ed. Oxford: Oxford University Press, 2016.

10

"I Spy with My Little Eye Something White!"

My Learnings as a White Pastor in a Minority Context

DANIEL T. SLAVICH

I WAS FRESH OUT of seminary and a few weeks into my ministry at an established Baptist church in South Florida, a church that had once boasted over 1,000 members and still had 60,000 square feet filling eight buildings on four acres. The working-class white community and congregation had long since transitioned, so that black people from Nigeria, Jamaica, and African America (which can be a very different America) filled up three-fourths of the neighborhood and congregation. The community's future, moreover, was clearly showing in the church's preschool, which had a few white teachers remaining but did not have a single white child enrolled except for my own.

A few weeks into my ministry in this context, I was walking through the courtyard between our buildings, next to one of our church's playgrounds. Two young black kids from our aftercare program, seated high on a play structure, were playing I spy. One of them said, "I spy with my little eye something white." Pause—and silence—until the second child piped up confidently, "Pastor Danny!"

I had not ever really thought of myself as white. I was just Danny. I was a Christian, a seminary graduate, and a family man; but I was basically average and normal, just like everyone else.

But not there. There, I was not just average, normal Pastor Danny. I was something white.

Now, I will not overplay my ignorance for rhetorical or narrative effect, because I understood that we lived in a society with different kinds of people. Growing up in Northern California, I recognized distinctions and diversities between myself, my Mexican American friend Junior in ninth grade, and my black teammate Lamont in Pony baseball. But I had never really thought about myself in racialized terms, that my racial identity had a meaning beyond just being "average" or "normal." In other words, I had never really thought of myself as a *white* person.

Yet as I began learning that I was not just an average, normal pastor, this unconscious ability to ignore the racial dynamics of my own identity began to dissolve. Instead, I started to learn what it meant that I was a white pastor in a community full of mainly black and brown people. That moment with those kids on the playground, and many moments in the following months and years, catalyzed a decade-long investigation. I read. I listened. I spoke, discussed, and even wrote a PhD dissertation on how the doctrine of the Trinity shapes the multiethnic church. In important ways, I wanted to learn what it meant that I was "something white." In important ways, I still want to learn; and in important ways, I am just starting my investigation. Then and now, I have longed to learn not just how to be a pastor but how to be a pastor in a racialized community. I long to learn how to lead a church in the way of Jesus. As I have stumbled along that narrow road, I have learned a few things about serving the church in light of the startling reality of being white.[1]

Before I get into some of my learnings from the last ten years, I want to ask you not to read what I am not writing. For everything I *will* say, I *could* say ten other things or add fourteen different nuances. While I trust that my theology is faithful to Scripture and that it frames this discussion, please realize that this is a personal reflection more than a biblical or systematic theology. As I narrate this personal reflection, I confess that I very much consider myself a learner rather than an expert in this space. I am aware that I risk being a bit like Andy Bernard in *The Office*, who took a truckload of women's studies courses at Cornell and considered himself an expert in feminism. Although Andy assumed he would know sexism when he saw it, he was quite obtuse functionally to the reality he thought he knew. Finally, please note that I am

---

1. I am not intentionally echoing the title of the helpful volume by the same title, which I will nonetheless note here. See Harris and Schaupp, *Being White*.

mainly addressing my fellow white brothers and sisters in Christ, who might benefit most from my learnings as a white pastor in a minority context. To share what I have learned, I will first briefly work to define what whiteness means in our social, cultural, and historical context. Second, I will draw out three implications I have learned about the meaning of being white. Third, I will give you four ways to put some shoes on this stuff and walk it out in your context.

What Does It Mean to Be a "White" Person?

Let me illustrate the meaning of being white by narrating some of my own family history. When my southern European, Scandinavian, and British family on both my mom's and dad's sides immigrated to America in the late eighteenth century, something shifted in the classification of their identity and thus of my own future identity. My great-grandparents were no longer just defined merely by their cultural, ethnic, national origins. Nor were they even just "American." As they moved into American social life and the marketplace, they quickly assimilated into a new identity—as white Americans. And to be a white American was not just a neutral descriptor. Whereas in European history, peoples and groups were Anglo or Saxon or French or Spanish or Italian or Russian or Scandinavian, our culture took one aspect of people of various European heritage and put them all in a category called white. This construction was based on a general sense of a certain color of skin tone, a certain heritage (broadly European), and a certain cultural context (again, broadly European). Those without these features, specifically physical features, were bucketed into other categories or "races," such as Indian or black.

We have to note here that the Bible does not give credibility to the idea of race in the sense that our culture has defined it for several hundred years. Scripture envisions a single human race united by the image of God. The Greek word γένος describes the created reality of kinds, races, or types of created realties.[2] All humanity is a single γένος (race). Yet, our Christianized culture sinfully and unbiblically came to define white as a supreme race of people who could not be legally enslaved and black as an inferior race of people who could be legally enslaved. Along with this, something like a spectrum between white and black (including Native American, Latino, and Asian) developed. Of course, this also entailed ideas of superiority and inferiority, normality and abnormality.

2. I first learned this point from my friend Steve Tamayo, who has written helpfully on this topic. See Tamayo, *Ethnic Identity.*

So, when that third-grader on the playground identified me, Pastor Danny, as white, he was commenting not merely on the tone of my skin. He instead was ascribing to me a historical truckload of other implications of being white in America. I learned to be aware of some of these implications as I navigated the leadership of a largely minority and black congregation in light of historical, social, and biblical realities. Three of these implications, which I will explore below, are the topics of privilege, politics, and power.

THREE IMPLICATIONS OF BEING WHITE

Implication #1: Privilege

The term *white privilege* generates much heat but often little light.[3] Most discussions do not accurately define the term, so here I will work toward a definition. Again, I will first illustrate the idea of white privilege with some of my own family's story. As my family moved into American culture in the first half of the twentieth century, their ability to assimilate into generally white American culture provided them with significant opportunities in employment, the marketplace, and housing. They were able to work very hard and accrue a modest amount of wealth. To recognize the reality of white privilege is not to say that my family was wealthy (they were not) nor to say that my family did not work hard for the life they were making (they did). Instead, speaking of white privilege recognizes that my family has a history of opportunities not

---

3. We find some of the themes discussed here, as well as above and below, in the literature on critical race theory (CRT), e.g., Crenshaw et al., *Critical Race Theory*. To some, any connection to CRT immediately places such themes beyond the pale of acceptable Christian discourse. Having read some of the most seminal literature on the subject, I tend to assess the CRT literature as having some helpful things in terms of diagnosis and some unhelpful things in terms of prognosis. Generally, I take an approach of "eat the meat, spit out the bones." As Israel did before the exodus, I believe the people of God can at points "plunder the Egyptians," while rejecting what we cannot learn from or appropriate in a way consistent with the logic of the gospel and the Scripture. Additionally, despite the inflamed rhetoric, much of what skeptics or antagonists of CRT call "CRT" is not, in fact, unique to CRT or actually CRT in any meaningful sense. Here, the analysis of Emerson and Yancey may instruct us more helpfully in *Transcending Racial Barriers*. The authors cast CRT as merely one of any number of paradigms of racial reconciliation and justice on a spectrum of sets and subsets of "dominant group obligations," with overlapping concepts such as white responsibility, anti-racism, reparations, Marxism, and the work of Cornel West (Emerson and Yancey, *Transcending Racial Barriers*, 30, 46–60). Similarly, they locate another cluster of paradigms of "people of color obligations" such as colorblindness, rejecting a victim mentality, conforming to Anglo norms, and valuing entrepreneurship in minority communities (Emerson and Yancey, *Transcending Racial Barriers*, 30, 33–45).

provided to the family of a similarly aged black man. Let's call this black man Ronnie, a name inspired by a black pastor friend of mine.

Ronnie's family was historically enslaved, accruing zero assets for their labor until Emancipation in the 1860s. For a century after Emancipation, Jim Crow laws made it difficult and often impossible for Ronnie's family to accumulate wealth and assets in the same way that my family was able to do. Ronnie's family was excluded from many of my family's opportunities for employment, marketplace entrepreneurship, and housing. When black communities did create such opportunities, they were often punished and terrorized back toward poverty, as in the destruction of Black Wall Street in Tulsa, Oklahoma, in 1921. Such a history helps to explain why the average black (or Latino) family in America has a fraction of the wealth of the average white family.[4] This historical reality is, in part, what white privilege means. White privilege means that cultural and physical features have led to a family history and present identity as white—an identity that has provided opportunities which a person who is black (or another minority) has not generally had in the same way until quite recently, relatively considered. Even now, looking at the number of important indicators of high-level positions of influence and earning power is instructive. The vast majority of CEOs, congressmen, senators, and presidents have been and are white. You can name on a hand or two the exceptions. These exceptions signal progress, but disparities still remain. For example, while my family quickly solidified itself as a middle-class household more than a century ago, Ronnie's family only became "solidly middle-class" within the last generation.[5]

With the context of this story in mind, I believe that my responsibility begins with recognition. I must recognize that our society has defined my family as white, and thus my family—and I—have benefitted from our society's wicked way of grouping people together in racial categories. If you are a fellow white person, you should recognize this pattern and how you may have benefitted from it. Likewise, we should learn how this pattern has disadvantaged—and still disadvantages—our black (and minority) neighbors and brothers and sisters in Christ. The idea that a dozen or more ethnic and national groups (from Europe) could be bundled together as "white" and defined as superior and not enslaveable, while another dozen and more ethnic and national groups (from Africa) could be bundled together as "black" and defined as inferior and enslaveable is at odds with the biblical vision of human

---

4. Bhutta et al., "Disparities in Wealth."

5. "Solidly middle-class" is Ronnie's own description of his family's economic story, told in a personal conversation.

dignity. More pointedly, as we have seen, this racializing has very real and present implications for different groups of people today.

Implication #2: Politics

In 2012, our church was a voting precinct, and folks lined up around the corner, 90 percent of them voting for Obama over Mitt Romney, including members of our church. This fractured my categories, because I had been brought up under the basic assumption that Democrats were so close to hell that their tie-dyed shirts smelled like smoke. But at my church I found fellowship and deep Christian relationships with genuine believers whose politics did not map onto the categories operating in my mind for a quarter of a century. For example, after a senior adult lunch one Wednesday afternoon, I helped a sweet older black woman in church carry her things to her car. She said, "Pastor, it's the grey Toyota with the Obama sticker." This woman loved Jesus, and she loved the Bible—and she had an Obama sticker on her Corolla. Another time, my wife and I were at the house of a couple from our church, a black man and a white woman. After dinner, we played a game in which a card is put into the middle of the table with an adjective, and everyone has to play a card from their hand that aligns with that description. During one turn, the card in the middle of the table read "stupid." As we each in turn flipped over our matching cards, someone showed this one: "George W. Bush." What startled me was the immediacy of the response. "Oh, that's a clear winner!" they said. The other cards had no chance, because for them "stupid" and "George W. Bush" was an obvious connection.

Now, my point here is *not* a political one. Instead, my point is that as a white pastor in a black community, my political vision had to be adjusted in light of cultural and community reality. Before these experiences, I would have said in theory that we shouldn't make the preaching of the gospel a partisan political moment. But as a child of the 1980s, raised by parents newly converted when I was two years old during the summit of the influence of the Moral Majority and the Reagan revolution, I also had running as software in the back of my mind that Christians were Republicans. I had to wrestle with the serious reality that I wasn't going to win anyone to Jesus with Republican politics. If I wanted our church to flourish in both unity and diversity, I had to make space for the nearly unthinkable: a Christian Democrat.[6] I needed space

6. I am not here denying the very robust and often fruitful movement of black and minority conservative and Republican voices. Nor do I imply that "real" black people vote Democrat or that conservative or Republican black voters or candidates are somehow beholden to "white supremacy." Such charges poison the air of our national, political, and

for Una to have an Obama sticker on her car and Jesus in her heart. I needed to affirm that our primal Christian political confession is that Jesus is Lord. I had to learn that any other prudential questions about political and governmental alignments must be clearly subjected to the lordship of Christ governing his kingdom through his church.

Implication #3: Power

White cultural norms die very hard, if they die at all. Here I was: twenty-eight years old and as green as a fresh Christmas tree; yet I was entrusted with the reins of this congregation. What were the circumstances of my receiving this charge, this authority, this *power*? I came from a middle-class white family that had been able relatively easily to facilitate my seminary education straight out of college. Without much trouble, I relocated myself 2,500 miles from California to Kentucky, driving I-40 in my Ford Focus. This ability for our family had not seemed exceptional, and from a certain perspective, it was not exceptional. We were not wealthy. We were a relatively normal, middle-class, suburban white family. But just that "normality" is a world more than I had ever realized. For example, we did not need to take out any loans for tuition or housing. I waited nearly six months to get a part-time job that I worked mostly to earn extra cash. My focus was getting educated and prepared. Then, when I was close to graduation, we connected to a friend who knew a friend hiring for a church. I was seen as ready, with the ink still drying on my MDiv diploma. Even though this church was more than half black, I was hired. Part of the context here was a cultural norm that saw education as a sort of credential for ministry. Part of the context was the fact that the church's culture remained largely white, even though the community and congregation itself had become black and brown. I realize that not everyone has the same opportunities for education and employment, that the very process of receiving education and finding employment is racially charged. You might say, "But I know many white people who didn't have those advantages you have described." Fair enough. But the point I am illustrating is one about the contrast between the relative ability of a white family to provide this sort of experience with the

---

theological discourse. I reject such mischaracterizations. Likewise, I do not intend here even to make any basic value judgments about any political party or platform (though I have decided opinions about these questions). Instead, I am merely making a more general point about population groups and constituencies that tend to align with one political paradigm over another, and the needed willingness of Christian communities to embrace political diversity, as well as ethnic, economic, and generational diversity.

ability of a black or brown family to do so. The point I am illustrating is the relative average power differential that can often result from such a disparity.[7]

I had been entrusted with power and authority, which was largely unearned. So, a year into my leadership, when I wanted to replace our worship leader with someone I considered more talented, I misunderstood when the previous worship leader, a black man from the Caribbean, felt slighted. In a church meeting, he referred to himself as "a professional black man." His comment struck me as unnecessarily racially charged. I was not trying to replace him because he was black. I was trying to replace him because I wanted someone with a different kind of musical and vocal range of abilities. I am ashamed to say that I muttered to one of our older, white deacons after the meeting that I was disappointed that this man had "played the race card."

But I wonder, now, if maybe there were power dynamics at play that I did not understand then. Surely, part of the dynamic was generational (he was older), and part of the dynamic was experiential (I was a year into my first pastoral role). But I also wonder if there was a sense in which this man, a dignified black man, had reason to feel slighted by a young white man two and a half decades his junior. He was in the midst of earning a doctorate in education, yet here I was with the great balance of power. Should I have recognized that not only experience, not only age, not only musical preferences, but also racial power dynamics could complicate such a situation? I think the answer is yes.

So, What Now?

In our church, every week, we ask and answer this question: "So, what now?" We think through the implications of our Sunday study of Scripture for our Monday through Saturday decisions and actions. Similarly, below, I want to draw out four ways to move forward in light of the discussion above.

Grow in Awareness

If you are a white leader, you likely need to spend twice as much time listening and learning as you do leading. You should realize that you might find

7. See "Born to Win." The study concludes, "Stunningly, a child from the bottom quartile of socioeconomic status who has high test scores in kindergarten has only a 3 in 10 chance of having a college education and a good entry-level job as a young adult, compared to a 7 in 10 chance for a child in the top quartile of socioeconomic status who has low test scores." Additionally, "the system conspires against young people from poor families, especially those who are Black or Latino. Among these youth, even those who 'make it' and earn a college degree are less likely than their more affluent peers to get a good entry-level job as a young adult."

yourself in positions of authority that you did less to earn than a corresponding minority leader in a comparable position. In discussions of authority, influence, or networks, assume you have blind spots that you, by definition, cannot see. A few years into my ministry at our church, I was still learning to learn about these matters. One of the most seminal and paradigm-forming volumes I read was *Divided by Faith*.[8] This was analogous to the Pixar film *Inside Out*, which explores the interior life of a young girl named Riley. If you have seen the film, you might remember the sort of islands of personality and understanding that Riley has in her mind. *Divided by Faith* rocked my categories, doing something like destroying old islands of understanding and raising new ones in their place, as I also engaged directly in life and ministry with my black and brown brothers and sisters. Whole new themes in Scripture changed from black and white to living dynamic color; from unnoticed—or barely noticed—to glaringly obvious; from theoretical and two-dimensional to real life, right in my very midst.

A few years into my ministry, preaching through Nehemiah, I came to Nehemiah 5, in which wealthy Israelites were drawing literally ungodly amounts of interest from the poor among them. I drew out the implications for wealth disparity in our own time and place. I noted that the average wealth for the typical white family was significantly higher than that of the average black or brown family. The many black folks in our congregation heartily rang out "Amen" and "That's right" and "Mm-hmm."

A few days later, an older white man in the congregation told me he was disappointed that I had brought up that point. "You're creating division," he charged. "I've always gotten along with all of *them*, but I couldn't believe so many people agreed with you," naming especially one black lady in our church. "I've known her for years, and I can't believe she would say amen to something like that," he said, shaking his head.

I responded, "Maybe you just don't know her as well as you thought you knew her."

Get Discontent

We need to cultivate a holy discontent with any form of injustice, never allowing any measure of comfort God may grant to us to wet the flames of holy desire for righteousness. If our minority brothers and sisters suffer, we suffer with them. If our brothers and sisters weep over injustice, we weep with those

8. Emerson and Smith, *Divided by Faith*.

who weep. We lament and we mourn. We pray, we fast, we grieve, yet not like the world, not without hope (1 Thess 4:13).

We should also be discontented to look around our congregations and executive leadership tables and see only white faces, finding bodies seasoned with salt but no pepper (or any number of other spices). Any nutritionist worth her salt (pun intended) will tell you that too much salt can gum up the lifeblood of the body, leading to clotting, strokes, and death. I believe with everything in me that God designed a multiethnic church of the nations, not just in a global, universal sense or an eschatological sense, but in a local sense. He wants local churches that look like heaven.[9] I also think that we need to consider whether historically black churches and immigrant churches might be the ones who need to lead the way in cultivating these kinds of congregations. To say it another way, white conservative Christians should be more discontented about injustice and segregated congregations than they are about their diminishing cultural influence.

Be an Ally

If you are a white Christian, recognize that God might have positioned you to influence the world and the church for the better. You likely have a measure of privilege and power, for all the reasons I discussed above. I am not talking about being a white savior. Our minority brothers and sisters are not helpless or in need of coddling. Instead, we need to ally ourselves by a posture of humility and apprenticeship in the way of Jesus. We need to learn and serve. Once, a group of folks from our church attended a seminar with a campus ministry that was open only to minority participants. I chafed at this, and quite honestly, I still feel fairly uncomfortable with it. That said, I am learning to be humble enough to recognize that certain dynamics at play make me say, "I don't really get it. I don't really like it. I'm not even sure I agree with it, but if you say you need this space, and it's better if I'm not there, I trust you." Love believes all things (1 Cor 13:7). White Christians need to love our black and brown brothers and sisters enough to believe them when they speak to us.

---

9. I lay out this argument more fully in Slavich, "In Church as It Is in Heaven." An early and profound influence on me here was the writing ministry of Mark DeYmaz. See DeYmaz, *Building a Healthy Multi-Ethnic Church*; DeYmaz and Li, *Leading a Healthy Multi-Ethnic Church*.

Get Uncomfortable

White Christians must willingly dislocate ourselves in terms of cultural and ecclesial comfort. We must be willing to stand with our brothers and sisters when they are right, even and especially when it might put us at odds with a conservative donor base. We must wander with a sense of political and ecclesial homelessness, realizing that our passport is ultimately issued from the kingdom of God and our primal political confession is that Jesus is Lord. This has nothing to do with charges of wanting to get published by the *The New York Times* or to receive the embrace of some group of secular elites. This has everything to do with loving our neighbors and with maintaining the unity of the Spirit in the bond of peace (Eph 4:1–6). Are we ready to count the cost? Candidly, I get weary of this whole discussion at times. Do we really have to talk about race? Can't we just preach the gospel? Then I think, "If I'm sick of talking about it, imagine how much my black and brown and Asian brothers and sisters are sick of living it."

CONCLUSION

As we consider the meaning of being white in a racialized and diversifying world, let us love well enough to believe, bear, and hope all things. Let us listen and learn. Let us humble ourselves in the presence of the Lord and in the presence of our Christian brothers and sisters. Let us cultivate churches that look like heaven, with Jesus in the middle of the congregation. Let us pray for grace, until that day when Jesus drops the new Jerusalem from the sky and makes all things new. Until then, let us learn to truly see those around us, to spy with our little eyes *all* those precious in his sight.

BIBLIOGRAPHY

Bhutta, Neil, et al. "Disparities in Wealth by Race and Ethnicity in the 2019 Survey of Consumer Finances." *Board of Governors of the Federal Reserve System*, 28 Sept 2020. https://doi.org/10.17016/2380-7172.2797.

"Born to Win, Schooled to Lose: Why Equally Talented Students Don't Get Equal Chances to Be All They Can Be." Executive Summary. *Georgetown University Center on Education and the Workforce.* https://files.eric.ed.gov/fulltext/ED599950.pdf.

Crenshaw, Kimberlé, et al., eds. *Critical Race Theory: The Key Writings That Formed the Movement.* New York: New Press, 1995.

DeYmaz, Mark. *Building a Healthy Multi-Ethnic Church: Mandates, Commitments, and Practices of a Diverse Congregation.* San Francisco: Jossey-Bass, 2007.

DeYmaz, Mark, and Harry Li. *Leading a Healthy Multi-Ethnic Church: Seven Common Challenges and How to Overcome Them.* Grand Rapids: Zondervan, 2010.

Emerson, Michael O., and Christian Smith. *Divided by Faith: Evangelical Religion and the Problem of Race in America*. Oxford: Oxford University Press, 2000.

Emerson, Michael O., and George Yancey. *Transcending Racial Barriers: Toward a Mutual Obligations Approach*. Oxford: Oxford University Press, 2011.

Harris, Paula, and Doug Schaupp. *Being White: Finding Our Place in a Multiethnic World*. Downers Grove, IL: InterVarsity, 2004.

Slavich, Daniel T. "In Church as It Is in Heaven: An Argument for Regenerate and Ethnically Diverse Local Church Membership." *Midwestern Journal of Theology* 16 (2017) 38–60.

Tamayo, Steve. *Ethnic Identity: Bringing Your Full Self to God*. LifeGuide Bible Studies. Downers Grove, IL: InterVarsity, 2021.

11

Between Memory and Hope

Filipinx American/AAPI Communities and the Leitourgia
for Justice, Belonging, and Identity

NEAL D. PRESA

Remember the Potawatomi, Sauk, Kickapoo, Meskwaki tribes,
on whose land the CPT conference meets.

AROUND THE TIME OF the COVID-19 shelter-in-place directives in the state
of California, there was a rising rate of hate against Asian American communities, spurred on by former President Donald Trump in his labeling of
the virus as the "Wuhan virus" or the "China virus." That descriptor served
to implicate all non-Hispanic, non-White, and non-Black people as somehow
responsible for the pandemic. This meant that all of us who looked—and who,
in fact, are—of Asian/Asian American descent were targets of some expression of hate. In response, on March 19, 2020, the Asian Pacific Policy and
Planning Council, Chinese for Affirmative Action, and the Asian American
Studies Department of San Francisco State University launched the Stop AAPI
Hate coalition. The coalition aggregates and reports incidents of hate against
Asian American and Pacific Islander (AAPI) communities.[1] From the period

1. See https://stopaapihate.org/about/.

March 19, 2020 to June 30, 2021, there were 4,548 reported incidents of hate in 2020 and 4,533 in the first half of 2021.[2] Types of discrimination involved any reported incident of verbal harassment, shunning, physical assault, civil rights violations, and online harassment.

A recent headline in the *The New York Times Magazine* captured what has been at stake for our AAPI communities—"The Myth of Asian American Identity"—with the pull quote, "We're the fastest-growing demographic group in the U.S. But when it comes to the nation's racial and ethnic divisions, where do we fit in?"[3] This long-standing reality of AAPI communities not having a clear identity in the American social landscape is exacerbated further and deeper by the immense contributions AAPI communities have given to the United States at great sacrifice to their personhood and their very lives. One simply has to be in a hospital to find that a majority of the nursing staff are Filipinos, the very frontline workers who are and have been combatting the COVID-19 coronavirus since its inception in America. These courageous workers continue to struggle today to care for the health and well-being of all patients regardless of citizenship status, racial identity, ethnic identification, and socioeconomic standing.[4] As the fastest-growing ethnic group within the AAPI communities, Filipino Americans have been, in many respects, the visible minority among invisible minorities. They have struggled as a diaspora community to remember, belong, and ultimately receive recognition. In short, it is a matter of justice.

Because Filipino Americans, both those who immigrated from the Philippines as well as those who are descendants of immigrants, are shaped and influenced by the Catholic and Protestant Christian traditions, this brief presentation seeks to locate the struggle for justice, belonging, and identity in the arena of faith. More specifically, the struggle to remember, and therefore to *re-member*, finds its impetus and empowerment in the locus of the church's worship of the triune God and derivatively in the comprehensive theology of life as *leitourgia*—the liturgy after the liturgy. In this brief presentation, I will discuss:

- The Filipino/Filipino American struggle in the midst of colonialism and post-colonialism

- The role of memory in healing and identity

- Life as *leitourgia* and how liturgy is the basis for a robust political theology for justice, belonging, and identity

2. Yellow Horse et al., "Stop AAPI Hate," para. 1.

3. King, "Myth of Asian American Identity."

4. Econar, "For Generations, Filipino Nurses."

This presentation is premised on the following: that justice and generational healing for the Filipino American communities require a retrieval and redemption of memory as framed from the standpoint of life as *leitourgia*.

THE FILIPINO/FILIPINO AMERICAN STRUGGLE IN THE MIDST OF COLONIALISM AND POSTCOLONIALISM[5]

An old adage describes the Philippines as being "three hundred years in a convent and fifty years in Hollywood." This is a description of the Filipino people as having been subjected to colonial rule by Spain, beginning in the sixteenth century until the late nineteenth century, followed by American imperialism into the mid-twentieth century. History books and classroom instruction teach the following:

- that the Philippines was "discovered" by Spanish explorer Ferdinand Magellan in the sixteenth century

- that the indigenous Filipinos who were regarded by their Spanish colonizers as "brutes and savages" needed to be civilized and Christianized

- that those same indigenous Filipinos were rescued from Spain by American troops in 1898

- that Filipinos were given a new way of life and more freedom with American military protection and the American cultural and economic life—both in the American presence in the Philippines and with Filipino immigration into the United States from the early twentieth century to the present

This linear history, similar to the New World of America being "discovered" by Christopher Columbus and Amerigo Vespucci as they sailed the ocean blue at the great expense of Indigenous peoples, neglects the oppression and subjugation endured by indigenous Filipinos and the resistance that Filipinos gave against Spain and then against America. Revisionist history that has been perpetuated for generations depicts Filipinos as needing to be saved, as wanting to be saved, as seeing Spain and then America as civilizing saviors. This revisionist history elides the painful struggle of indigenous Filipinos who fought for independence, who desired to retain their livelihood and heritage, and who—in the process of resistance—were subjugated and subjected to foreign influence and made to feel inferior.

---

5. For a more detailed history than the one sketched here, see chapter 2 of Ocampo, *Latinos of Asia*, 15–34.

The US policy doctrine of manifest destiny, buttressed with such notions as American exceptionalism, justified a westward expansion from the original thirteen colonies to the frontiers of the nascent United States of America. Regarding the country as originating from the blessing of divine providence, American policymakers and the American psyche understood America—as codified in the Declaration of Independence and the US Constitution—as a shining beacon to the world, a "city on a hill." As such, the land annexations and expansionist impulses of America translated into the purchase of erstwhile Spanish colonies at the end of the Spanish-American War: the Philippines, Guam, Cuba, and Puerto Rico. Here, the US policy of manifest destiny partnered with Spain's imperial ambitions to possess the Philippines's natural resources and to continue the Catholic Church's missionary impulse to propagate Christianity. For the United States, manifest destiny provided the justification for economically benefiting from the Philippines's natural resources, its geopolitical strategic location in east Asia and the Pacific, and its additional land to expand Protestant missions.[6]

What is missing from this chronicle of colonizer and colonized is the struggles of the Filipinos themselves. Far from this being a simplistic 400-year history of transfers of power from one global superpower to another, the true history of the Philippines involved the actual lives of indigenous Filipinos such as the Igorot, Bagobos, Moros, among many others, who were commodified, objectified, and monetized for the gains of both church and state, to the detriment of their native way of life. For example, in the Philippine-Spanish War of 1898, when for nearly five years Filipinos fought for their independence against Spain, they enjoyed a short-fought freedom until American forces confronted Spanish forces at Manila Bay. Textbook and classroom stories of the Battle of Manila Bay (pejoratively called the "Mock Battle of Manila Bay") depict American Admiral of the Navy George Dewey defeating the Spanish Navy, when, in fact, the reality was that Spanish forces were cornered by advancing Filipino forces on land and American forces from the sea. Spain's emissary negotiated a deal with Commodore Dewey that Spanish forces would pretend to surrender to American forces so that Spain would not fall to the indigenous Filipinos, whom they viewed as brutish and uncivilized savages, and by whom defeat would be a global embarrassment to the erstwhile superpower.

When American forces later defeated Spanish forces in the Battle of Manila Bay and treaty negotiations were conducted in Paris between Spain

---

6. President William McKinley called for the "benevolent assimilation" of the Philippines, exhorting Methodist church leaders in 1898 to evangelize the Philippines, unmindful of the fact that many Filipinos were already Christian due to the preceding 300 years of Catholicism's presence with Spain's colonial footprint. See this account in Gonzalez, *Filipino American Faith*, 37.

and the United States, Filipino representatives at those treaty talks tried to prevent the sale of the Philippines to the United States. The Philippines was treated as a bartering chip between two global powers. And even after America acquired the Philippines and established it as a protectorate of the United States, Filipinos continued their resistance against the new American colonizers, resulting in thousands of Filipino deaths. The low regard that America had of Filipinos was depicted at the 1904 World's Fair in St. Louis, Missouri. The largest exhibit at the fair was a forty-seven-acre site featuring indigenous Filipinos like the Igorot, near naked and described as dog-eaters.[7] The fair occurred during military battles between American and Filipino forces in the Philippines, broadcasting the message to fair attendees that such uncivilized savages needed to be civilized, thus justifying a war being perpetuated halfway around the world. When the United States defeated Filipino forces, Filipinos were allowed to immigrate to the United States, and, with the onset of the second World War, thousands of Filipinos served in the US Armed Forces. Following World War II, and with the granting of Philippine independence by the United States in 1946, American colonialism in the Philippines ended in some respect, and immigration came to a halt. The second wave, in about 1965, occurred during the Civil Rights Movement in the United States. At that time, the United States was experiencing a labor shortage in such sectors as the healthcare industry, with American immigration policy limiting the number of immigrants from China and Japan. What is not widely known is that Filipino labor activist Larry Itliong joined forces with Mexican labor activist Cesar Chavez, and together they advocated for higher wages and better working conditions for farm workers. Throughout this time, Filipinos were regarded as the "other" or as a "model minority" within the social and racial upheaval taking place in American society.

7. Sieber, "'Savages' in the White House."

Ad depicting Filipinos at the 1904 World's Fair

For Filipino Americans, the essence and sense of *kapwa* (communal in-terrelatedness, "I am because of you," a concept similar to the Zulu sense of *ubuntu* in South Africa) meant that their hearts and minds were connected to both the Philippine homeland as well as the plight of Filipinos in the Ameri-can diaspora.[8] This dual commitment of *kapwa* exacerbated the difficulty of not feeling fully connected to American society, of not belonging to this new

---

8. See Presa, *Ascension Theology and Habakkuk*, for more on this dynamic of *pakikibaka* (struggle) as it is lived out through *kasamahan* (togetherness) and *bayanihan* (unity through service). This dynamic is the essence of *kapwa*.

land, and of being otherized by White America. Stephen Cherry observes the duality and expansive nature of community for Filipino Americans:

> Their (Filipino Americans') communities have no fixed geographic boundaries. They are just as connected to their regional provinces in the Philippines as the American suburbs in which they physically reside. . . . Most scholars agree that people in general, not just immigrants, are influenced by the community in which they live or were raised, but few recognize that they are simultaneously members of multiple communities that function in varying degrees of harmony or discord with each other. This produces a host of competing forces that shape their public and civic life. It also influences how people define and build their senses of community.[9]

The Americanization of the Philippines served to convince Filipinos that anything or anyone that was from the Philippines—people and products—was not as sublime as anything or anyone from America.[10] For instance, it became ingrained in the mind and heart of native Filipinos that their dark or brown skin was inferior to the white or lighter complexion of Americans. This was reinforced by commercial media, pop culture, music, television, and cinematography, and with the advent of the internet age the messaging was broadened through social media. The American ideal as seen through the lens of Hollywood was glamorized and idolized. And a communal psychology began to develop of belittling fellow Filipinos who tried to be American but whose distinguishing features of skin complexion, lingual accent, and inability to connect socially with American-born Filipinos—let alone white America—led to them being further ostracized with such labels as FOB (fresh off the boat). To survive and to try to assimilate (as opposed to integrate) into the American culture, there was a high priority to learn the English language. Indigenous Filipino languages were replaced with English instruction in all grade schools, colleges, and universities in the Philippines. In short, whether in the Philippines itself or in America, Filipinos found a ubiquity of American influence upon their identities and a near total displacement of being Filipino.

THE ROLE OF MEMORY IN HEALING AND IDENTITY

Memory plays an essential role for psychological health. One may desire to repristinate pleasant, life-giving events of the past or avoid unpleasant and

9. Cherry, *Faith, Family, and Filipino*, 54–55.
10. David, *Brown Skin, White Minds*, xix.

traumatic past events. Sometimes, unpleasant memories can resurface, re-traumatizing victims and stifling their psychological growth. In both cases, whether one desires to relive or avoid memories, past events influence and shape our present conditions and choices for the future, whether we are aware of it or not—whether we consciously choose or not. Memory also plays an important role in helping to heal from past trauma. The late Brazilian philosopher and educator Paulo Freire asserted that what is needed for those oppressed by trauma is for victims to *conscientize* their struggle through the elements of naming, reflection, and action.[11] But this becomes more difficult if one cannot remember the trauma.

An emerging field of psychology is known as colonial mentality (CM). Colonial mentality was pioneered by Frantz Fanon in 1961. Colonial mentality has more recently been used by Filipino psychologist E. J. R. David of the University of Alaska at Anchorage and his doctoral supervisor, Sumie Okazaki, to analyze the plight of Filipino Americans, a plight similar to Native Americans/Indigenous Americans following two centuries of European occupation. David and Okazaki describe CM as an "internalized oppression" that causes one to believe that their ethnic heritage is inferior to Western culture and whiteness, resulting in "uncritical rejection of anything Filipino and . . . uncritical preference for anything American."[12]

The perpetuation of CM cannot be countered because of the collective amnesia of the Filipino history of struggle and the revisionist history from American educators and educational institutions that elide the painful truth of the past in order to maintain the veneer of American exceptionalism.

Colonial mentality psychologists point to Freire's insight in the difficult and essential work of decolonization, in which the trauma of truth and the truth of trauma are brought to the consciousness of the oppressed by the oppressed themselves, so they can express how the internalized past has adversely affected them personally and collectively. We remember Jesus's words in the Gospel according to John, "And you will know the truth and the truth will make you free" (8:32 NRSV).

Healing cannot occur until there is critical reflection regarding the *what*, the *who*, the *why*, and the *how*—to wit, conscientizing the source and cause of the trauma. Who are the oppressors and perpetrators? Who are the ones called to bring about change? Why must change occur? How will that change be realized? Such critical reflection must include the difficult steps of naming and identifying the internalized oppression, including the generational paralysis that resulted from the systemic and institutional oppression that

11. Freire, *Pedagogy of the Oppressed*.

12. David and Okazaki, "Colonial Mentality Scale," 241.

prevented the victims from mounting an effective psychological, political, economic, and spiritual resistance to the trauma.

When Catholic Christianity arrived in the Philippines in the sixteenth century with the Spanish conquerors, the church was allied with the Spanish state; there was mutual interest in the expansion of the state's interests and the church's power under the pretext of gospel expansion. The alliance of military, political, and economic interests with that of the church created a formidable partnership in which indigenous Filipinos and their heritage became dominated or altogether replaced. The hegemony of Spanish, and then American, power slowly eroded the indigenous Filipino heritage, including indigenous Filipino spirituality that had shamanistic, animistic elements; active agency of ghosts and spirits; and a robust sense of the spiritual world. In its place was an emphasis on the oral/spoken word, the written word, and doctrinal and dogmatic instruction, i.e., on the cerebral and intellectual aspects of faith development and formation.

Because the Philippines, for nearly five centuries, had the largest population of Catholic adherents per capita next to Vatican City, Filipino Americans are shaped and influenced by that Catholic faith, even if they are (or become) Protestant Christians or leave the Christian church altogether. The question for our purposes, then, is: Are there elements in the Christian faith that carry the framework and seeds for the retrieval of memory? Are there structures inherent within the Christian faith that actually enable and empower naming, reflection, and action, but which may themselves have been co-opted, ignored, or abused of their efficaciousness to bring healing and wholeness for Filipino Americans? This presentation asseverates that the power and possibility of liturgy enable the work and witness of justice, specifically the theology of *leitourgia* as public work for the benefit of the common good. This public work, which is itself lifelong, involves every facet of life, including a key structural and theological dimension of the liturgy: the anamnesis—the remembering in order to be re-membered (a concept discussed more in depth later). It is in the anamnetic dimension of the church's worship and the Christian life that we are in communion with Jesus Christ, in communion with the triune God, and in communion with the ancestors of the faith and of our heritage, both the living and the dead. Further, the anamnetic aspect of the Christian faith and of Christian worship helps Filipinos and Filipino Americans to remember the Philippine homeland, to remember our commitment to live faithfully as diaspora Filipinos in our American home, to remember the living God and God's love, to remember our ancestors in every time and in every place, and to be in communion with the saints of the faith. In remembering, we are re-membered or made more part of the entirety of the body.

LIFE AS *LEITOURGIA* AND POLITICAL THEOLOGY

The word *liturgy,* or its adjectival form *liturgical,* connotes for several Christian Protestant traditions—particularly evangelical traditions—images of icons, incense, robed clergy, pipe organs, Gothic cathedrals bedecked with stained glass windows, and a gathered assembly facing the chancel. These same traditions, more iconoclastic in their theological and ecclesiastical sensibilities, emphasize the centrality of Scriptures with the prominence of the physical presence of the Bible at the chancel, the central positioning of the pulpit at the chancel, and the allocated time given for the spoken word/sermon relative to other parts of the worship service. The late liturgical historian James White helpfully reminds us that all Christian traditions are liturgical, because liturgy and liturgical in their etymologies and history are about a public work or service rendered for the benefit of the common good. In the enactment of such an act, the ones doing the work have a deeper appreciation and recognition of their part in the community and the body politic. For early Christian communities in the Roman Empire, *leitourgia* (liturgy) was the Roman public works systems of building dams, repairing roads, and maintaining the waterways. Those who performed such work for the benefit of the community saw that they belonged to the empire and that, in doing the work, their citizenship in the local and broader community of the empire was enhanced. Early Christian communities appropriated that term and that concept to Christian worship generally, and specifically and most supremely at the Eucharist or the Lord's Table—the liturgy. James White avers that all Christian traditions are liturgical in that they are worshipping, praying to, and praising God for the benefit not only of the gathered assembly and not merely for Christians but, beyond that, for the entirety of the world. For White, it is not a question about whether a church is liturgical, but about whether it is characterized as "high liturgy" or "low liturgy." The former denotes the so-called "smells and bells" of incense thuribles, robes, and formal processions in stained glass churches. The latter is composed of spontaneous prayer and song; a worship service centered around the spoken word; and music involving drums, guitars, and stages (and perhaps even beach balls, lights, and smoke machines!).

For centuries, Christian communities regarded the centrality of the Lord's Table as the embodiment of liturgy, and therefore the table marked off that community as being liturgical, because life itself was liturgical. Orthodox liturgy designates life from Sunday through Saturday as the Liturgy of the Liturgy, to indicate that life lived outside the gathered community was done as an act of worship: "Present your bodies as a living sacrifice, holy and acceptable to God, which is your spiritual worship" (Rom 12:1 NRSV).

Because the Lord's Table was a sacramental feast that converged spoken word, the physicality of food and drink, the sacramental (or real) presence of the Lord Jesus Christ, a meal ordained and instituted by the Lord himself, and the communing of God's people with God and with one another, the Lord's Table was the preeminent place of the divine-human encounter, the triune God with the redeemed. In the Orthodox traditions, the table was itself heaven-on-earth in a sacramental and real dimension where, through the agency of the Holy Spirit, the gathered assembly is brought into the very throne of God and the prayers of the faithful are lifted to the heart of God. Key to the struggle for justice is that part of the Lord's Table liturgy called the *anamnesis*, "Do this in remembrance of me."

Anamnesis, from which the English word amnesia is derived, is about remembrance and memory. In one dimension, anamnesis is about retelling and recounting past events, like looking at old photos of family camping trips and partaking in the mixed emotions that go with the retelling and hearing of those past events. But there's an even deeper understanding of anamnesis in the Judeo-Christian tradition from our Jewish forbears. Anamnesis has more to do with living memory, being connected to past events as if we were there or being in communion with the people and places of those past events, because those stories are family stories that live on still, that impact and shape our present choices for the future. So, when African and African American slaves sang the old spirituals—"Go down, Moses, way down in Egypt's land! Tell ol' Pharaoh, 'Let my people go!'"—those prayer songs did not merely recount the Old Testament chronicle of the Israelites' exodus from Egypt. Nor did they merely infuse them with hope that those stories spoke about present-tense deliverance. Nor did they merely serve as coded-language messages to other African and African American slaves to actually go down to a designated river to escape from their slaveholders' clutches. The spirituals did all of that, with one additional salient action: they invoked the Spirit of God and the spirits of the ancestors of the living and the dead to bring that present community to the delivered community of the Israelites, to sacramentally bring them to Israel, with Moses, with the Israelites in their exodus because their exodus is our exodus. We are on that desert journey crossing the Red Sea. Anamnesis is about the convergence simultaneously of past-present-future precisely because the living God, the Spirit of God, is not bound by time and space and is the Person who unites God's people—the living and the dead—with the living God and with one another.

Liturgical scholar Bruce Morrill connects the political theology of Johann Baptist Metz to liturgical theology in showing the efficacy of anamnesis to the work of justice in the public sphere. Metz saw that when Christian gatherings celebrate the Lord's Table and recount the events of Jesus Christ's life, culminating in his death and resurrection—*mortis et resurrectionis Jesu Christi*—in the *memoria passion* (remembering the passion), Christian believers are being called by the Lord to continually be connected to his struggle, his pain, and his salvation. For it is through his very death and his very life that the struggle is justified and redeemed. And through that communion with the struggling Savior who is victorious, who himself is in solidarity with a suffering and struggling world, we are redeemed, and we are empowered to bear witness to the Savior in the public sphere.[13] Metz's political theology was premised on the notion that the *memoria passion* of Jesus was a public act. His judgment before Pilate was a revolutionary act, as he was confronted by the political and religious authorities in the public theater of public opinion. His penalty of crucifixion was, likewise, a public act, and subsequent testimonies of the apostolic messengers were public confessions to magistrates and public figures. Whenever worshipping communities recount Jesus Christ's life, death, and resurrection, lifting up praises and prayers for and from the world, they are engaging in that anamnetic activity of remembering the Lord and remembering the world and the world's needs. These acts are revolutionary deeds that counteract a world that would rather relegate a crucified Savior to the outskirts of the city, away from the centers of power, a world that would rather not serve the hungry and clothe the naked—the very people whom Jesus Christ loved and for whom he declared the kingdom of God had come.

Methodist theologian William Willimon wrote more than a generation ago on the efficacy of worship as pastoral care in a book with the same title.[14] Willimon, whose scholarly work is on pastoral theology and pastoral ministry, observes that the primary locus for pastoral care and healing is in the context of worship, where God's people engage with the resources of the faith and through which God heals. Applying the insights of psychologist Paul Pruyser on diagnostic variables, Willimon sketches the gifts of worship for healing of the mind, body, and spirit: awareness of the holy, prudence, faith, grace, repentance, communion, and vocation.[15] Willimon notes, too, that pastoral care and healing cannot fully occur apart from worshipping communities of faith. Through the liturgical rites of Christian worship, the love of God and the prayers of God's people are brought to bear on the hurt and injustice in the world. Ritual theorists and anthropologists buttress this point. The living encounter of God's people occurs through ritual action and ritual performance, where the chaotic world is somewhat ordered and understood and infused

13. Morrill, *Anamnesis as Dangerous Memory*, 32–36.

14. Willimon, *Worship as Pastoral Care*.

15. Willimon, *Worship as Pastoral Care*, 65–71.

with meaning. We are reminded, too, that ritual can wreak violence and cause chaos. In both cases, there is meaning-making that occurs.[16] For Christians, and for Filipino American Christians specifically, the ritual act of worship, the prayers offered, and the bread/cup received at the Lord's Table have salutary effects in mending hearts, speaking to the memories of the wounds of the world, the wounds of our ancestors, and the wounds of our Holy Ancestor, Jesus the Christ.

Filipino American spirituality, both that which was grounded in indigenous spiritualities and the Christian traditions to which many of us belong, has in itself the robust anamnesis that Metz describes. As mentioned above, indigenous Filipino spiritualities had an active sense of the agency of spirits/Spirit, of interacting with ancestors, of living memory in hope. The Filipino essence of *kapwa* corresponds to the Christian notion of *koinonia* (fellowship/communion)—that the person understands their personhood to be inextricably linked to the wider community. "I am because we are." Consequentially, the wider community's well-being is my well-being. This also means that for *kapwa* to be retrieved, collective memory needs to be revived. For in remembering the struggle of the ancestors—of our ancestors—we redeem the Filipino-ness of who we are, our identities even as diaspora Filipinos. To decolonize oppression, subjugation, historic and systemic discrimination that instills inferiority in our Filipino heritage involves the very tools that colonizers have given: the very liturgy that re-members us to the Savior, to the Spirit, to the communion of saints of the living and the dead. In other words, the very tools that colonizers used to elide or replace Filipino culture can be used by Filipinos in transformative, redemptive ways for justice, belonging, and identity for Filipino communities.

The work of decolonization begins with remembering the truth, naming the truth. Filipino scholar Leny Strobel describes the praxis of decolonization. It involves sharing the narratives of one's life, particularly the aspects of struggle. Narrative in the praxis of decolonization is "a search for cognitive knowledge about Filipino and Filipino American history and culture; a positive confrontation with the emotional aspects of this process; and a search for a new way of constructing knowledge in a language that weaves together the various aspects of decolonization."[17] Decolonization involves dignifying the storied narratives of the oppressed. Strobel asserts that narratives "use memory to trace their [Filipino Americans'] collective development as a people." Citing the insights of Mikhail Bakhtin, Strobel asserts that "oral traditions are recalled and infused into the new narratives, creating . . . 'a double-voiced

16. Driver, *Liberating Rites*, 26, 132–33.
17. Strobel, *Coming Full Circle*, 96–97.

discourse'—a dialogue of two voices, two worldviews and two languages . . . to transform the present, in particular, power relationship between dominant and dominated, rather than to create nostalgia for a past."[18] The result will be "a larger narrative for a community's identity."[19] Strobel describes the "generative themes" in the decolonization process:

- The Affective Content of Decolonization
- The Power of Naming and Telling
- The Role of Language
- The Need for Filipino Cultural and Historical Knowledge
- The Role of Memory
- Imagining the Filipino American Community: New Expectations and Visions
- The Process of Building Community Institutions
- The Generational Responsibilities
- Educational Expectations
- The Gender Issue
- The Role of Filipino Spirituality[20]

Each of these themes involves arduous, sustained praxis that calls forth the prayers, creativity, imagination, energy, resilience, and solidarity within and beyond the AAPI communities and the Filipino and Filipino American communities. Strobel goes further in describing the essential and necessary role of orality in Filipino culture, the telling and retelling of memory that is transformative and redemptive. She asserts: "The process of reclaiming Filipino history as a counter narrative to the history written by outsiders becomes a process of reclaiming one's memory."[21] She goes on to explain the salutary effects of the counternarrative: "The recovery of language, of one's voice, of one's

18. Strobel, *Coming Full Circle*, 63.

19. Strobel, *Coming Full Circle*, 64.

20. These eleven dimensions are similar to the nine transformational practices characterized by "justice, love, reconciliation, and peacemaking" in Kim and Hill, *Healing Our Broken Humanity*, 14. The nine practices, in brief, are "reimagine church, renew lament, repent together, relinquish power, restore justice, reactivate hospitality, reinforce agency, reconcile relationships, recover life together."

21. Strobel, *Coming Full Circle*, 120. I am grateful to my colleague in ministry and fellow Filipino American pastor theologian, The Rev. Dr. Gabriel J. Catanus, for underlining this point for me and redirecting my attention to Strobel's distinctive way in expressing the power of narrative and memory.

story, is re-created in the memory. There is a sense of turning in one's soul through the power of language and imagination."[22] But it is not just about the individual. As noted above, the essence of being Filipino can be summed up in the word *kapwa*.[23] *Kapwa* means that an individual's identity is best and fully understood in relation to the family, to the *barangay* (village), to the larger community. Thus, Strobel goes further: "To reclaim memory at the personal level, is to engage in the process of creating a collective memory with a people's history" and forming a connection "to the past where people have participated in resistance to colonization and have done heroic deeds."[24] Strobel's approach to memory is similar to Metz's *memoria pasionis*: the retrieval of memory is subversive and revolutionary and therefore, to use Morrill's description, "dangerous," because the memory does not merely recall a past event and heal the trauma of colonization and oppression; the retrieval of memory redeems and provides the oppressed the means by which the past trauma of colonization is vanquished. In the *leitourgia*, the struggles of Filipinos are connected with Jesus the Christ, who was the victim of powers and principalities that sought to stamp out God and the kingdom of God; Jesus' very body, which was terrorized, violently colonized, so to speak, invaded with human hatred through hammered nails on a wooden tree, becomes the Oppressed and Colonized One who is in solidarity with oppressed Filipino communities. Which means Jesus' freedom from his struggle on that Easter morning is the very source of a counter-revolution of freedom that is made possible by Filipinos' own memory retrieval of resistance.

Korean American clergywoman and theologian Grace Ji-Sun Kim reminds us that the work of justice, reconciliation, and healing "begins with our wounds. . . . We need to have the courage to enter the places of our greatest pain in order to be instruments of peace in the world."[25]

In remembering the struggle, we remember those who were, have been, and are not only allies in the struggle but co-conspirators on the journey of hope.[26] We would do well to remember the closing part of the words of institution in the eucharistic liturgy from 1 Cor 11:26: "When we eat this bread and drink this cup, we proclaim the Lord's death until he comes again." In

---

22. Strobel, *Coming Full Circle*, 120.

23. See Presa, *Ascension Theology and Habakkuk*.

24. Strobel, *Coming Full Circle*, 120.

25. Kim, *Embracing the Other*, 152.

26. I am indebted to my colleague in ministry, The Rev. Laura Mariko Cheifetz, for coining the term "co-conspirator" to designate not only an ally in the struggle but one who invests oneself at great risk because of a passionate desire and commitment for justice to be done.

doing so, Kim adds that we need to account for the psychological and spiritual affects and effects of trauma by tapping into the "dark abyss of our erotic power. . . . Erotic power produces both conflict and resolution."[27] Kim utilizes the concept of eros love that Spirit God infuses in us to indicate the deep intimacy "through the subjective engagement of the whole self in relationship. . . . The erotic underlies all levels of experience and compels and propels us to be hungry for justice at our very depths."[28] Spirit God is who animates people to confront and struggle with the pain and trauma of the other and through whom the stories of one another's lives are dignified and redeemed.

We remember the Lord's death not merely as a past event but as an encounter with the living Lord in our midst, who struggles with us and with whom we struggle—an encounter with the Holy One who struggled with holy love for this broken world. He remembers us, never leaving us nor forsaking us, and re-members the broken Filipino bodies and souls, restoring us Filipinos and Filipino Americans as beautiful creatures created in the image of our Asian *kapatid* (brother), Jesus the Christ.

BIBLIOGRAPHY

Cherry, Stephen M. *Faith, Family, and Filipino American Community Life.* New Brunswick, NJ: Rutgers University Press, 2014.

David, E. J. R. *Brown Skin, White Minds: Filipino-/American Postcolonial Psychology.* Charlotte, NC: Information Age, 2013.

David, E. J. R., and Sumie Okazaki. "The Colonial Mentality Scale for Filipino Americans: Scale Construction and Psychological Implications." *Journal of Counseling Psychology* 53 (2006) 241–52.

Driver, Tom F. *Liberating Rites: Understanding the Transformative Power of Ritual.* Boulder, CO: Westview, 1998.

Econar, Fruhlein Chrys. "For Generations, Filipino Nurses Have Been on America's Frontlines." *CNN,* 8 Oct 2021. https://www.cnn.com/interactive/2021/10/health/filipino-nurses-cnnphotos/.

Freire, Paulo. *Pedagogy of the Oppressed.* 30th anniv. ed. New York: Continuum, 2000.

Gonzalez, Joaquin Jay, III. *Filipino American Faith in Action: Immigration, Religion, and Civic Engagement.* New York: New York University Press, 2009.

Kim, Grace Ji-Sun. *Embracing the Other: The Transformative Spirit of Love.* Grand Rapids: Eerdmans, 2015.

Kim, Grace Ji-Sun, and Graham Hill. *Healing Our Broken Humanity: Practices for Revitalizing the church and Renewing the World.* Downers Grove, IL: InterVarsity, 2018.

27. Kim, *Embracing the Other,* 152.

28. Kim, *Embracing the Other,* 141.

King, Jay Caspian. "The Myth of Asian American Identity." *The New York Times Magazine*, 5 Oct 2021. https://www.nytimes.com/2021/10/05/magazine/asian-american-identity.html.

Morrill, Bruce T. *Anamnesis as Dangerous Memory: Political and Liturgical Theology in Dialogue*. Collegeville, MN: Liturgical, 2000.

Ocampo, Anthony Christian. *The Latinos of Asia: How Filipino Americans Break the Rules of Race*. Stanford, CA: Stanford University Press, 2016.

Presa, Neal D. *Ascension Theology and Habakkuk: A Reformed Ecclesiology in Filipino American Perspective*. New York: Palgrave MacMillan, 2018.

Sieber, Karen, "'Savages' in the White House and the 1904 World's Fair." *Theodore Roosevelt Center at Dickinson State University* (blog), 6 July 2019. https://www.theodorerooseveltcenter.org/Blog/Item/Savages%20in%20the%20White%20House%20and%20the%201904%20Worlds%20Fair.

Strobel, Leny Mendoza. *Coming Full Circle: The Process of Decolonization among Post-1965 Filipino Americans*. 2nd ed. Santa Rosa, CA: Center for Babaylan Studies, 2015.

Willimon, William. *Worship as Pastoral Care*. Nashville: Abingdon, 1982.

Yellow Horse, Aggie J., et al. "Stop AAPI Hate National Report: 3/19/20–6/30/21." *Stop AAPI Hate*. https://stopaapihate.org/stop-aapi-hate-national-report-2/.

12

Justice and Memory

GREGORY THOMPSON

Cain spoke to Abel his brother. And when they were in the field Cain rose up against his brother and killed him. Then the Lord said to Cain, "Where is Abel your brother?" He said, "I do not know; am I my brother's keeper?" And the Lord said, "What have you done? The voice of your brother's blood is crying to me from the ground."

GEN 4:8–10 ESV

THE INVENTION OF MEMORY

ON A GENTLE SPRING night in May of 1924, the white citizens of Charlottesville, Virginia, gathered for a parade. Standing in the shadow of Thomas Jefferson's mountain home and dressed in their finest, the men, women, and children of the white community waited expectantly for what was to come. As the sun began to set, their waiting found its answer as several hundred men, dressed in white robes and—in some cases—with masked faces, began to march in torchlit procession toward the heart of the city. As they did so, the gathered crowd greeted them with cheers and songs, their faces illumined by the light of the passing fire.

This evening march was just one part of an entire week of celebration that included gala dinners, minstrel shows, all-day screenings of the film *Birth of a Nation*, and opulent evening balls. All of this, however, was in service of the week's culminating event: the unveiling and consecration of a new statue of Robert E. Lee in the heart of Charlottesville's downtown. And so, on the morning of May 21, hundreds of community members—professors, judges, attorneys, soldiers, Klan members, fathers, mothers, and pastors—gathered in the newly created Lee Park for the event. And together, many of them in tears, they cheered as three-year-old Mary Lee—great-granddaughter of the general—pulled the cord to unveil the statue, revealing the horse-borne image of one who, the presiding official said, was "the greatest man who ever lived."[1]

This event was not unique. In Charlottesville alone, this was one of four statues erected between 1919 and 1924: Lewis and Clark (1919), George Rogers Clark (1921), Thomas Stonewall Jackson (1921), and finally, Robert E Lee. Each installation was attended by similar forms of celebration. But these events were not just in Charlottesville.[2] To the contrary, they were simply reflective of larger movements across the nation. From roughly 1880 to 1930, in communities across the nation, Americans erected nearly 6,000 memorials—overwhelmingly to Confederate soldiers. And in so doing, they transformed not only the American landscape but also America's account of itself—its public memory. Why? Why did this incredible and historically unique period of memorialization take place? To answer this question, we need to understand the cultural context in which these memorials emerged.

After the Civil War, the American nation faced two fundamental cultural challenges. The first of these was determining the political and social status of newly emancipated African Americans. The second was establishing a basis upon which the South and North could reintegrate into one nation. From 1865 to 1877, the answer to both questions was to reconstruct the American South into the shape of the Constitution and to create a society in which African Americans and white Americans alike could share in the rights of democracy. The basis of unity was, in other words, *constitutional*. We were seeking to be a diverse people held together by a constitution.[3]

This basis, however, did not endure. Because of constant resistance to Reconstruction in the South and a shift of priorities in the North, Reconstruction came to an end in 1877. And with it, any vision of a universal American

1. Nelson, "Object Lesson," 27–28.
2. Nelson, "Object Lesson," 18.
3. For more on this initial strategy, see Foner, *Reconstruction*.

identity anchored in the Constitution. In its place emerged a new basis of American unity, namely, a *cultural* basis of unity—a shared self-concept of who "we the people" actually are.[4]

To understand the features of this cultural self-concept, one need only look at the statue of Lee erected in Charlottesville all those years ago. What does it show us? It shows us a man—and through him, a people—characterized by the following: racial purity (Lee fought to resist racial equality); Christian piety (Lee believed that God had called him into this work); personal liberty (Lee believed in the rights of Southerners to live free from federal intervention); military agency (Lee was willing to defend these beliefs with violence); and civilizational triumph (in the end, even in defeat, Lee emerged as triumphant).

It is important to understand that this is not simply a statue. *It is an instantiation of a cultural self-concept, the articulation of an aspirational vision of who we are as a people.* And not only that, this cultural vision of what it means to be an American is one in which both Southern and Northern Americans could find themselves. Each understood itself as white. Each understood itself as deeply Christian. Each understood itself as committed to liberty. Each understood itself as militarily powerful. Each understood itself as part of the best civilization in the world. In other words, even though the South and the North disagreed with one another and held one another in suspicion—and if our electoral map is any indication (and it is), they still do—they could both find themselves in this statue and in the cultural vision it represented. And in finding themselves in these categories, they also found one another. *This cultural vision—a vision of self-righteous, libertarian, militaristic, imperialistic, male whiteness—became the new cultural basis for American unity.*

Indeed, it became the basis of a new form of public memory, a new way of interpreting American history. And from 1880 to 1930, this new public memory remade the American landscape in a lasting way. As the 2021 *National Monument Audit* produced by the Philadelphia-based Monument Lab reveals, of the nearly 60,000 memorials in the United States today: nearly 90 percent are of white men; nearly 6,000 of them are Confederate memorials, maintained to the cost of $40 million in public funds; fewer than 10 percent are people of color of any kind; fewer than 6 percent are women; nearly 35 percent depict military conflict and conquest; and fewer than 1 percent depict enslavement and/or abolition.[5]

---

4. For more on the development of a *cultural* basis of reunion, see especially Blight, *Race and Reunion*, and Varon, "UVA and the History of Race." See also Foner, *Second Founding*; Lears, *Rebirth of a Nation*; and Kyle and Roberts, *Denmark Vesey's Garden.*

5. Allen et al., *National Monument Audit*, 19, 25, 27.

These memorials are features not only of the American landscape but of the American public memory. Indeed, the invention, legitimization, and perpetuation of a certain version of American public memory are their very purposes.

THE VIOLENCE OF MEMORY

But as important as the stories that are told, the memories that are valorized, are the stories that are not told—the memories that are set aside. It is important to remember that white men were not the only people living in America at that time. To the contrary, and to use just one example, African Americans were also a part of this nation. And as a part of this nation, they built its economy; contended for its political integrity; bore arms in its wars; and definitively shaped its intellectual, institutional, culinary, and artistic culture. And yet, in this new postwar American renarration, the truths about African Americans were simply erased from the story. These truths? The dignity of their humanity. The crime of their abduction. The violence of their subjugation. The endlessness of their captivity. The rape of their bodies. The significance of their labor. The sale of their children. The desperation of their resistance. The courage of their flight. The resilience of their communities. The shrewdness of their institutions. The brilliance of their art. The power of their religion. The legitimacy of their demands. The triumphant gorgeousness of their mere survival. Where, one asks, are the monuments to these? In the white supremacist mythology of postwar America, the answer is nowhere.[6]

And not only were these stories not told; they were actively erased. This, you will remember, is the very same period as the rise of Jim Crow laws in the American South. It is the very same period in which anti-black race riots took place in nearly forty cities across the nation. It is the very same period in which over 4,000 African Americans were lynched. Put most succinctly, as memorials to white soldiers went up, African American communities were torn down.[7]

This violent erasure, this "willed forgetting," reveals something deeply important about the nature of American racism. Its aim was not, fundamentally, to hate African Americans; its aim was, rather, to *not see* them. Its aim was to render their humanity and its claims upon white Americans invisible. This is why white America cloaked blacks in the guise of inhumanity, why it hid their labor behind walls, directed them to hidden staircases, banished

6. For more on this, see Kwon and Thompson, *Reparations*, 71–82.
7. Nelson, "Object Lesson," 19.

them to separate restrooms and schools, zoned them to different neighborhoods, excised them from children's textbooks, and buried them in unmarked fields. America did not want to see.

And this was the goal of the racist renarration of postwar America: to erase everything that did not serve the narrative of white supremacy and fill the resulting emptiness with spectacular and beguiling monuments designed to distract white Americans from the depth of their collective self-deceit.

This simultaneity of festive memorialization and brutal violence is not accidental. To the contrary, it is reflective of the twinned malignancies at the heart of the American public memory: romanticization and erasure. The simple truth is that America is a nation that systematically destroys the lives of nonwhite people, erases what we have done, and then builds monuments to our own genius on top of the very graves of those whom we have harmed. And this—this—is the foundation of our public memory. It is a memory that is at once utterly fictive and irrepressibly violent.

THE GOD WHO REMEMBERS

This brings us to our passage. It is a story of two brothers: each made of God, loved by God, and gifted by God with particular gifts to be used to honor God and serve one another. But—in a scene repeated daily around us—this fraternal difference became threatening. And the threat led to resentment. The resentment led to violence. The violence led to erasure. Cain, the first practitioner of violence, is also the first practitioner of violent memory; for he not only murdered his brother, he sought to create a new reality in which his brother was forgotten.

But God is a God of memory. A God who remembers—even in the face of the wickedness of our willed forgetting. So, he remembers Abel. And in remembering, he comes. And in coming, he says to Cain, "Where is your brother?" This, like all of our Lord's questions, is an invitation—in this case, an invitation to memory. But Cain rejects this invitation, clings to his illusion of forgetfulness, and says, famously, "I don't know. Am I my brother's keeper?" These are the most famous words. But the most important words are what God says next: "I hear your brother's blood crying out from the ground."

This is one of the first justice passages in the Bible. And its horizon is memory. Cain murders his brother and seeks to bury what he has done in the mists of forgetfulness. But God remembers, and in remembering, he makes known. And because of this, all these years later, you and I sit before the memorial of this passage and remember.

Justice and Memory

Over the course of its long and complex history, the American church has given itself to the work of racial justice in a host of ways: through the pursuit of political representation and legal equality, through the struggle for educational equality and economic development, and through the practice of relational reconciliation. And we should do so. Each of these is a critical dimension of the work of confronting racial injustice.

But one of the most important horizons of the church's work in confronting racial injustice is curiously neglected: the horizon of memory and memorialization. However, a very powerful case could be made that this public memory—these memorials around us—actually legitimate and sustain the very racial injustices that we seek daily to eradicate. To put it another way, even as we fight racial injustice at the local courthouse, we leave the town-square memorials that sanctify that injustice in place.

Because of this, I believe that one of the most important ways in which the Christian church in America can—and should—confront racial injustice is through the work of redemptive memorialization, the work of listening to those voices buried beneath the ground and making them known. Indeed, I believe that we will never heal until we do so. We were, after all, there when the original memorials—monuments to violence and self-deceit—were erected. And we must be there when the new—and true—memorials are erected in their place.

The Work of Memory

But how? I know well that to speak of the redemption of public memory may seem vague, and the work of memorialization may seem unfamiliar. Indeed, this is the type of work that—insofar as we think of it at all—we leave to museums, mural artists, and local governments. And I understand this. But I also understand that to ignore this critical work is to leave one of the most important avenues for our healing to others. Because of this, I believe that one of the central tasks of the church, in its struggle for racial justice, is to step deliberately and creatively into this work of public memory and memorialization, to go into our communities and to tell the stories of those whose memories have been buried underground.

But how? While this work will take many forms and will, of necessity, vary from community to community, there are, in my judgment, five critical characteristics of this work that can guide the church as it undertakes the redemption of public memory. First, this work is *remedial*. Because a large part of the American church remains deeply ignorant about its own cultural history, our work begins with learning the truth and, subsequently, telling the truth. Second, this work is *local*. The work of storytelling happens best when it is focused on the hidden stories of our own local communities. Third, this work is *collaborative*. It begins by centering other voices, listening to their stories, and laboring together to tell the truths we find. Fourth, it is *creative*. It is important to remember that the myths of postwar America found their most powerful expression in works of public art such as statues, films, plays, and novels. In like manner, the redemption of our memories must also express itself creatively, aspiring to redeem our imaginations and to heal our memories. Finally, this work must be *enduring*. Because we are seeking to overcome the violent myths of history and to replace them with the truth, we must give that truth its own perpetual and protected status through the work of public memorialization.

If, in its pursuit of racial healing, the Christian church gives itself to the work of renewing our public memory, and does so in accessible ways that are remedial, local, collaborative, creative, and enduring, then we will make an unimaginable contribution not only to the healing of our collective memory but also to the transformation of our collective future. We did so once, with dark result; and we may yet do so again in the pursuit of light.

The Future of Memory

In 2017, the nation watched in horror as—once again—white citizens marched through the streets of Charlottesville in torchlit parades. Their destination— and the site of all the violence that you witnessed on television—was the statue of Robert E. Lee erected nearly 100 years before. This was—as all racial conflicts are at their heart—a conflict waged at the fault lines of public memory. And, after four years, enormous pain, and the polarization of a city—the Robert E. Lee statue (along with all three others) was removed in the summer of 2021. And now, as we walk daily by the empty spaces created by this removal, the question facing each of us is: What story will take its place?

The answer to this question is deeply controversial and still unknown. But what is, in my mind, uncontroversial is that the Christian church must be a part of this work of nurturing a renewed public memory. We are, after all, the people of a God who remembers. And in his name, part of our calling is to hear the voices that call out from beneath the ground and to devote ourselves to making them known. For it is only in this way that we will contribute to a future in which not only our communities but our very memories are, at last, made just.

BIBLIOGRAPHY

Allen, Laurie, et al. *National Monument Audit*. Philadelphia: Monument Lab, 2021. https://monumentlab.com/audit.

Blight, David. *Race and Reunion: The Civil War in American Memory*. Cambridge, MA: Belknap, 2001.

Foner, Eric. *Reconstruction: America's Unfinished Revolution, 1863–1877*. New York: Harper Perennial, 1986.

———. *The Second Founding: How the Civil War and Reconstruction Remade the Constitution*. New York: Norton, 2019.

Kwon, Duke L., and Gregory Thompson. *Reparations: A Christian Call to Repentance and Repair*. Grand Rapids: Brazos, 2021.

Kyle, Ethan J., and Blain Roberts. *Denmark Vesey's Garden: Slavery and Memory in the Cradle of the Confederacy; A 150-Year Reckoning with America's Original Sin*. New York: New Press, 2018.

Lears, Jackson. *Rebirth of a Nation: The Making of Modern America, 1877–1920*. New York: Harper, 2019.

Nelson, Louis P. "Object Lesson: Monuments and Memory in Charlottesville." *Buildings & Landscapes* 25 (2018) 17–35. muse.jhu.edu/article/723148.

Varon, Elizabeth R. "UVA and the History of Race: The Lost Cause through Judge Duke's Eyes." *UVA Today*, 4 Sept 2019. https://news.virginia.edu/content/uva-and-history-race-lost-cause-through-judge-dukes-eyes.

Index

Index

Index

Index

Manufactured by Amazon.ca
Bolton, ON

35687105R00113